CREATIVE ARTS
WITH OLDER ADULTS

A Sourcebook

CREATIVE ARTS WITH OLDER ADULTS

A Sourcebook

CO-EDITORS
NAIDA WEISBERG, M.A.
!Improvise! Inc.
Providence, Rhode Island

ROSILYN WILDER, Ed.D.
New York University, New York

HUMAN SCIENCES PRESS, INC.
72 FIFTH AVENUE
NEW YORK, N.Y. 10011

Copyright© 1985 by Naida Weisberg and Rosilyn Wilder
Published by Human Sciences Press, Inc.
72 Fifth Avenue, New York, New York 10011

Printed in the United States of America
987654321

LIBRARY OF CONGRESS CATALOGING IN PUBLICATION DATA
Main entry under title:

  Creative arts with older adults.

  Bibliography: p.
  Includes index.
  1. Ages—Mental health services. 2. Arts—Therapeutic use. I. Weisberg, Naida. II.
Wilder, Rosilyn.
RC451.4.A5C74 1984   618.97′6891654   83-22602
ISBN 0-89885-161-0
ISBN 0-89885-163-7 (pbk.)

We dedicate this book

To making connections through the creative arts;

To so many of the older adults with whom we have been connected through the years.

Our parents who aged as gerontocrats;

The firm and infirm with whom we have worked in many places;

Those who have given us so much of insight, courage, love, and hope;

Friends, family and colleagues.

We hope this book will make a difference for the future.

ACKNOWLEDGMENTS
AND APPRECIATION

From Naida Weisberg

First of all, to my husband and friend, Al, a renaissance man, who said, "Do it!" and never stopped supporting the effort with wise counsel, generosity, and humor, as well as picture-taking.

To my children: Martha, who knew the problems before I did through her work with elderly; David, for his perceptive questioning and ability to empathize; Abby, for her quick eye and fresh response to the work.

To the members of my workshops and the staff of Briarcliffe Health Care Facility, Fruit Hill Day Care Center, the Jewish Community Center and Bethany Home, who continue to inspire me.

To my partners in !IM-PROVISE! Inc., without whom I cannot imagine my career.

To Dr. James Barsky for his generous advice throughout.

From Rosilyn Wilder

To my "support network": husband-sculptor Ben Lieberman — merciless critic, tireless advisor, and constant advocate; our children: Julie Lyonn Lieberman, violinist and author/composer, for eagerly shared expertise; Jeannie and Joe Scoglio for the vitality of their insight.

To my elder friends at the Essex County Geriatric Center and elsewhere for revealing many of the truths inherent in this book; and to the Essex County Division on Aging and County Executive Peter Shapiro whose support has allowed me to explore living meanings of the creative arts in gerontology.

To Drs. Nellie McCaslin, Patricia Rowe, Jerrold Ross, Frances Aronoff, Doris Berryman at New York University and Audrey Faulkner at Rutgers University.

To our contributors who have eagerly shared their expertise and revealed their commitment to the creative process with older adults.

To Norma Fox who first perceived the significance of this volume; to Jacqueline Sunderland for her astute comments on the work-in-progress. And to our typists, Lorraine Theroux in Rhode Island, and Jan Smith in Massachusetts.

To administrators of sites where this book took shape, including Jacob Edwards Library, Southbridge, MA; Yale Medical Library, New Haven, CT; Stockbridge Library, Lenox, MA; Mayflower Inn, Washington, CT; Broadknolls, Lenox, MA

CONTRIBUTORS

Marilyn Barsky, Ed.D. Clinical Psychologist, Orlando, Florida

John Belcher, B.S. Musician and Workshop Leader in nursing homes and senior citizen centers in Providence, Rhode Island.

Victoria Bryan Executive Director, Stop-Gap Theatre, Laguna Beach, California.

Stanley Cath, M.D. Associate Clinical Professor of Psychiatry, Tufts University School of Medicine, Boston, Massachusetts.

Laura Fox Founder-Director, Taproot Workshops, Setauket, Long Island, New York.

Paula Gross Gray, Ed.D. Gerontology, Activities Director, Jewish Home and Hospital for the Aged, New York City.

Pearl Greenberg, Ed.D. Professor, Fine Arts, Kean College, New Jersey.

Jocelyn Helm, M.A., DT, Director of the Princeton Resource Center, Princeton, New Jersey.

Delight Lewis Immonen, RMT M. Music Education, Musician/Music Therapist in nursing homes and senior citizen centers in Rhode Island.

Dorothy Jungels, B.A. Art; Dancer, Illustrator, Workshop Leader in nursing homes and senior citizen centers in Rhode Island.

Georgiana Jungels, A.T.R., Director of Art Therapy Studies, State University College, Buffalo, New York

Marc Kaminsky, M.A. Summa Cum Laude; M.S.W. Hunter College School of Social Work; Co-Director of the Brookdale Institute on Humanities, Arts and Aging, of Hunter College, New York.

Don Laffoon, M.A. Theatre, Co-Founder and Artistic Director, Stop-Gap Theatre; Laguna Beach, California.

Marian D. Palmer, RMT, B.S. Music Therapy; Midwest Speaker/Consultant to nursing homes.

Rose Pavlow, M.A., R.D.T. Creative Drama; Co-Founder of !IMPROVISE! Inc., a nonprofit corporation of Creative Drama Specialists in Providence, Rhode Island.

Gail Porter, B.A. Photography; Photographer-in-Residence. the Rhode Island State Council on the Arts, Providence, Rhode Island.

George Sigel, M.D. Associate Clinical Professor of Psychiatry, Tufts University School of Medicine, Boston, Massachusetts.

Carol Cavan Sinatra, M.S. Psychology, Drama Therapy Specialist Stop-Gap Theatre, Laguna Beach, California.

George Warner, Certified American Lineage Specialist, Hagerstown, Maryland.

Naida D. Weisberg, M.A., R.D.T. Educational Drama; Co-Founder of !IM-PROVISE! Inc., a nonprofit corporation of Creative Drama Specialists in Providence, Rhode Island.

Rosilyn Wilder, Ed.D., R.D.T. Director, ENCOMIUM Arts Consultants, Inc., Montclair, New Jersey.

ADMINISTRATORS AND EDUCATORS

Jeannette DelPadre, Program Coordinator, Scalabrini Nursing Home, North Kingstown, Rhode Island.

Audrey DuPont, Activities Director, Briarcliffe Health Care Facility, Johnston, Rhode Island.

Robert A. Famighetti, Director, Gerontology Center, Kean College of New Jersey, Union, New Jersey.

Lilly Miller, Director of Continuing Education, Goldfarb Institute; Educational Coordinator, Central New Jersey Jewish Home for the Aged.

Daniel M.O'Connell, Artistic Director and Fund-Raiser, Berkshire Artisans Gallery and Workshop, Pittsfield, Massachusetts.

Judes Ziemba, Activity Coordinator and Volunteer Coordinator, Heritage Hall Nursing Home (South Building), Agawam, Massachusetts.

CONTENTS

EDITORS' PREFACE

The time has come to openly acknowledge the role of the creative arts in the helping professions, to shatter the negative myths of aging in the 20th century, and to give more credence to the wisdom, experiences and needs of the long-lived. We have designed this book in the interest of an improved quality of life and a closer connection with living for all older adults and for you who live and work with them. Society is ready to accept aging as a natural time of life, not to be ignored, derided, or feared. And across the country, creative arts and arts therapy practitioners are demonstrating the effectiveness of their work in contributing to the mental health of the well elderly and to the reintegration of the alienated and depressed.

We wish to share a commonality of ideas and purposes as expressed by some of these diverse experts in gerontology and the creative arts, including both arts therapists and artist-educators. We hope to guide you to dig into and examine *many* art forms in order to discover how the arts overlap, interweave, and alternate in organic response to the special requirements of individuals and groups. You will find a feast of ideas which can be adapted to your own situations. We hope you will be inspired to prepare your program offerings with a zestful combination of these ingredients.

You will find approaches and techniques that encourage people to think, initiate, do, and communicate. Throughout these chapters are the kind of connections our writers make with their groups: listen for their excitement behind the methodology; the humor, the sharing, the spirit that can lift even the depressed or discouraged to smile. Detect the *high* of leadership that causes individuals to *turn on*—a mutual giving and taking.

The contributors to this volume offer noncompetitive programs that stimulate and promote individual participation in a cooperative group. Each builds an atmosphere of acceptance and trust—in which feelings are expressed and problems addressed on behalf of the healthy, normal facets of every individual. There is almost always some degree of wellness to be cultivated so that participants derive pleasure from the experience, and from the new respect engendered among group members.

At this writing, many of the dynamic, funded programs which serve life-enhancement, including those in the arts, are seriously threatened. Some have already been sacrificed along with scores of other human services. And yet there are more than 24 million persons, over age sixty-five; by the year 2000, it is projected there will be 32 million. Can so vast a population be denied expression? As their numbers grow, so too does their struggle to be fully acknowledged as worthy citizens linked inseparably to the mainstream of the nation.

Creative arts services can make a measurable contribution in enabling the aging adult to articulate desires, necessities, and aspirations. We believe—we know—the arts are potent resources for both the well and ill. We know this because we live it in our work in community settings and in institutions.

Historically, the arts and creative expression have challenged individuals to articulate the substance of life and to reaffirm their existence. An octogenarian sculptor, Edna Eckert, confined to her home, told us, "I think creative people are often long-lived because we are always re-inventing life; what we did yesterday we create anew tomorrow. Inherent in this process is *hope*."

And now the challenge moves to you, our readers. We hope this book will call forth, renew or reinforce your commitment to more significant, expressive, and restorative programming through the arts with older adults. Furthermore, we hope that through the implementation of this programming, you will find personal excitement and rewards for yourselves to help sustain meaning in your work and in your lives.

> *How good is man's life, the mere*
> *living! how fit to employ*
> *All the heart and the soul and the*
> *senses forever in joy!*
> Robert   Browning

Art . . . is a concrete living expression of the lives which have created it and, thereby, a connection to tomorrow.

Stanley Cath, M.D., Associate Clinical Professor of Psychiatry, Tufts University, School of Medicine; is a Lecturer in Psychiatry at the Boston University School of Medicine. He is a founding member and Vice President of the Boston Society of Gerontologic Psychiatry; Founder and Director of Family Advisory and Service Treatment Center. He is in private practice of psychotherapy, analysis, and geriatric psychiatry. Dr. Cath is the author of *Some Dynamics of Middle and Later Years* and *Institutionalization of a Parent — Nadir of Life* and co-editor with Dr. Martin Berezin of *Geriatric Psychiatry: Grief, Loss and Emotional Disorders in the Aging Process.* He is an editor of *Father and Child: Developmental and Clinical Perspective* published by Little, Brown, Inc. in 1982. Dr. Cath is a member of the American Psychoanalytic Association, American Psychiatric Association and the American Geriatric Society.

INTRODUCTION
EMPATHIC CONNECTIONS
Stanley H. Cath, M.D.

Landscape of the Soul

Very few things do not change in our lives. However, deep within us, certain core experiences contribute to an ongoing nuclear sense of self. Our earliest bonding and rupturing experiences consolidate either into a feeling of cohesiveness and pleasure, or contrariwise, may set into motion various protective devices we all use so as not to be hurt by loving and trusting.

All our lives the landscape of the soul is, or is threatened to be, littered with the debris of our search for others to complete and comfort our idealized or disillusioned relationships, as well as shattered dreams. Thus, by midyears, a balance is struck between aspirations fulfilled and goals never reached.

Then, with time pressing ever on, whatever personal integrity and gratification has been achieved may be lost. Disability or illness may be superimposed upon ordinary disappointments. Our abilities to grieve for our losses and to recover from them may be outweighed by our burden of depletion.

Tension and Apprehension about Life

Every person lives his or her own personal coefficient of tension and apprehension about life, the inevitable changes therein, and his or her own decline, depletion, and death. Ideally, in the course of dealing with stress and disruption, each infant, child, and adult learns to use innate "givens," genetic endowment, talents and skills to best advantage. In my work with long-lived people, I have found a range of character types, various life styles, and above all, unique responses to the crises of disability, disease, depletion, and death. In the passage from the evanescent to the senescent phases of life, three fairly distinct groups emerge.

19

Gerontocrats and Gerontophobes

The first and rarest are the gerontocrats. Such people rarely need our aid, for they live long, well, and beautifully. Some have skill in their hands, others in their heads; some are creative, others just industrious. Like Thomas Jefferson, they move from one interest or career to another without pause, doubt, or apparent pain. At the other extreme are the gerontophobes for whom life's end-phases carry unspeakable horrors.

And in between are most of us, the ordinary people, who struggle, may need help, and only rarely feel creative. For the last two cohorts the main task of living-long becomes consciously how to hold the self together.

Accordingly, the task for the creative therapist is how best to aid this process in different people with multifaceted personalities and resources. It often turns out that the crucial issues are not just the facts of disease, that is, illness or wellness; but the coefficient of tension associated with relating to people, then living with the self-image as it is confronted by the repeated later-life inventories of self-other and self-object assessments. Has one loved more than one has hated? Has one created more than one has destroyed? Can one feel there is something of worth left behind to mark one's having been? Are the answers tolerable, or do they create so much tension that one would rather decathect thinking, doing, creating, and even remembering, in toto?

Those who are not gerontocrats, and who lack the capacities to soothe the self or to rationalize away imperfections and disappointments, often acquire particular tendencies toward helplessness and depression which may make life unbearable. Some people's lives reflect either an avoidance of closeness and intimacy or a search for it with varying degrees of success. In especially vulnerable people with the so-called narcissistic disorders of self, regression follows each hurt or failure, and self-esteem plummets to earth. But in most people we can be certain there exists the wish not to be alone and the wish to reach out to others. The question is how to find the right key, how to find the door into which it will fit, and finally, if permitted to enter, how to make an empathic connection. For our purpose there must be time; we need to provide a place and create a method designed for the person at hand.

Art and Connectedness

Art, in its protean forms, tends to span time and space, and in so doing, assures humankind of its connectedness with the past, while seeming to promise an immutable and indefinite, rather than finite, future. It may well be that art does not communicate the same thing to different people. But I suggest that it may convey the same message to all: *it is a concrete living expression of the lives which have created it,* and thereby a connection to tomorrow. It is this connectedness revived which seems to define and affirm living, while it *defies destiny.*

It is generally believed that emotional deprivation and/or physical abuse are the sources of much pathology. It happens all too frequently that a painful contributor to high levels of anxiety, discomfort, and lack of motivation is an inflated sense of expectations from others, expectations not perceived to belong to the self. These idealized goals are often linked to performance and exhibitionism, i.e. the mother with musical aspirations who always wanted a career in opera, and whose son was chosen to live out that dream for her. Parental praise and approval may have taken the form of unrealistic idealization, leading to a sense of a false self, with much ambivalence about achievement and the creative use of the self. Thus we encounter another group of people who are "wrecked by success," never satisfied with how well they do or with the demands placed upon them. Some, possessed by "object hunger," remain involved in searching for approval, and are easy to contact and work with, while others resolve their uncertainty about who wants what for whom by various forms of schizoid withdrawal.

In the world of drama, dance, art, and music, illusion plays a pivotal role. In the process of aging, the retention of necessary illusion is precariously balanced with bitterness and disillusion. And if in the face of loss and restitution "man can still sing," one merits the title of gerontocrat. Those who cannot, we can help to sing — that is exactly what the authors in this book aim to do. In addition, they hope to bring a more fulfilled life not only to the long-lived, but to those who care for them. The making of connections then needs to be appreciated in all its complexity. Through art we make connections over time with all of those who have gone before, and who have struggled to express yearnings and "presumptions to matter"; we connect ourselves with our most primitive but enriching, soothing memories or schemata so deeply engrained as to be beyond words; and we reconnect with those who are here now and attempting to cross the all too often inhospitable desert between generations.

In our melting pot of nationalities, this wasteland has been even more eroded by mobility, inappropriate concepts of independence, and rapid obsolescence. By becoming carriers of an international language — the creative arts — understood by humans of all ages, isolation may be assuaged, the veil of protective withdrawal may be lifted, and old, almost forgotten sources of pleasure revived.

Our interventions must be designed to help our patients and clients come to the realization that they deserve more than they allow themselves to have ...
The goal must be to help reconnect troubled elders so they regain their self-esteem. . . . The Creative Arts may be unique in facilitating reconnectedness, the goal of any successful intervention.

George Sigel, M.D., Associate Clinical Professor of Psychiatry, Tufts University, School of Medicine; is a Staff Psychiatrist at the Tufts New England Medical Center and Director of the West Broadway Unit, Bay Cove (Tufts) Mental Health Center. He is the Chairperson of the Geriatric Task Force of Bay Cove (Tufts). Dr. Sigel is the author of numerous articles and a forth-coming book. He is a member of the Boston Society for Gerontologic Psychiatry.

FOREWORD

WHY DO SOME OLDER PERSONS DISCONNECT?

George Sigel, M.D.

So many troubled elders suffer from a pervasive feeling of being worthless and disconnected from the world around them. Many feel that they have lost all value and therefore have no claim on a health professional's time. No one modality of treatment is adequate in helping them; a range of options must be considered. Psychotherapy is only one of many tools that can be used to help this group *reconnect* and become participants in treatment to ease their suffering, prolong their lives, and add substantially to the quality of their lives.

The creative arts, because they rely largely upon nonverbal techniques, provide other tools that all clinicians ought to be aware of, if the pervasiveness of depressive illness among the elderly is to be adequately addressed.

Nobody Important

Many elderly persons feel they are "nobody important;" which reminds me of a passage from John Gardner's *Dragon, Dragon,* a children's story about the aged cobbler who came to the king's meetings and stood in the back of the room because "he had a feeling that since he was nobody important, there had probably been some mistake and no doubt the king had intended the meeting for everyone in the kingdom except him."

To effect the analogy, many elderly share the cobbler's feeling that the invitation to meet with the king must be a mistake. Or, in our own terms, when approached by any type of health care provider, these elders are apt to feel that they do not deserve the help; the worker is certainly in the wrong place, or clearly wasting his or her time with them. Elderly patients troubled with emotional problems will attempt to convince the worker that this time can be spent elsewhere with more worthy and certainly more deserving patients.

Ageism

Ageism, the subtle but pervasive attitude that defines the many ways the elderly are discriminated against, is a pernicious process that begins when people are young. Indeed, *Dragon, Dragon* is a children's storybook. And, sadly, the negative attitude that young people adopt toward the elderly persists even while people themselves age. In other words, as people age, they become members of the group they hold a prejudice against. *We all become "the elderly."*

This ageism, practiced also by the elderly, will greet us all as we approach elderly patients. They will often try to discourage our interest in them, or assume that our task of evaluating them is odious to us. Many elderly, especially those with some emotional troubles, will assume that we, too, despise them as much as they despise themselves. Often they will treat a therapist with scorn as they project their low self-esteem and self-contempt. Even if they are friendly and compliant, they will share very little in the interview, based on their conviction that there is little, if anything, to share.

When we are greeted this way by elderly patients who are referred to us for services, we can be easily sidetracked. Prompted by some of our own unsettled feelings about aging and the elderly, we are apt to maintain our own distance, to allow ourselves to be easily discouraged, or to rationalie a treatment approach that avoids intimate probing contact. We are likely to suggest that *others* implement a more supportive approach; at the same time, we ourselves can agree to a course that precludes insight, and that may at times suggest countertransference, acting out of our own needs to avoid a patient's pain.

Often, for this reason, a therapist will agree to see a patient, at the patient's suggestion, only once a month, a format that would really preclude psychotherapy. Seeing a patient once or twice a month can be helpful. However, such treatment plans do at times reflect a patient's low self-esteem and a counter-therapeutic alliance to avoid a more intimate contact that could result in the sharing of very painful and intense affects.

The Referral

Evidence that this attitude toward life and the elderly reflects ageism practiced by the elderly, is the pervasiveness of depression in this group. Depression is by far the most common emotional problem that afflicts the elderly, and often results in a mental health referral.

When a referral is made, the referring agency will often be aroused because of a precipitating crisis and want something done immediately. The needs of the referring system may often be different from the needs of the patient. The mental health professional will then feel an enormous tension between these conflicting needs. The evaluator will have to withstand the pressure from the agencies and/or families to "do something" quickly, and give the patient and the "situation" enough time so that a complete evaluation may be performed. One does not easily make friends when called in to do a mental health evaluation, because often the situation has festered to such an extent that the referring party demands a speedy solution. The task is difficult and challenging.

Agency and family resistance to the evaluation process is not the subject of this paper. It must be acknowledged, however, because it will often define the context into which the mental health professional must step in order to greet the patient and begin the task of evaluting his or her clinical situation and needs. The patient will often be quite passive in the presence of intense system pressures, demonstrating a compliance that usually reflects depression and lowered self-esteem, the problem the evaluator must assess. The system will, in other words, incorporate ageism, and will be reflective often of the treatment that the elderly patient believes he or she deserves. So even the health care system can begin to relate unkindly, at times abusively, to elderly patients.

When approaching such patients, the evaluator must be calm, thorough, and persistent to an extent that is rarely called for with younger patients. The responses of the elderly patients may range from compliancy to an "I'll take care of you, dear," attitude, to hostility and an overt but ambivalent rejection of you and your interest. Mild depressions are seen, as is psychotic illness with or without delusions and/or hallucinations. In between these extreme behaviors and diagnoses lie a host of variations and subtle resistances. In its most extreme form, there is the suicidal patient, and the known high rates of suicide among the elderly.

Case Histories

Mrs. B is a woman in her seventies who reportedly was confused, bizarre, and unable to care for herself. The quality of the initial referral suggested much concern, but also reflected that this "elderly" woman (and it was assumed that she was in her late eighties, not early seventies!) was obviously suffering from dementia and needed residential placement. When I visited her in her home, I was surprised to find a woman considerably younger than the referral sources had stated, and amazed to discover that there was no evidence of organic brain disease.

Her apartment was in deplorable shape, and it was clear that she and her landlord were in a struggle that she was losing. While pleasant, she was clearly depressed, and as she briefly told me her life story it became clear that she felt her present situation was no more nor less than she deserved. She expressed the sentiment that maybe another apartment would do better, but that this one was acceptable. I was enraged, and tried to understand why she was not.

Her landlord had hired some men to help her clean and they had stolen many of her possessions. She accepted this without anger and with a tolerance that was shocking. She described how her bathroom was difficult to use because water would often pour down from upstairs. The way this was told, one might have thought it was a delusion. As I mulled over this possibility, water began to pour down from the ceiling. She pointed to it as if it were a perfectly normal event that one had to accept and live with: One gets what one deserves.

Mr. D is a ninety-five year old man who refused service from any of the agencies. His middle-aged nephew apparently would beat him up from time to time. This elderly man did not want to get his nephew in trouble, and felt that the abuse he received was a small price to pay if the nephew was protected. Completely absent was a sense of rage and indignation that would define a normal range of self-esteem, that could translate into a firm rebuff of his nephew with an assertion that this uncle deserved and would demand better treatment. Like Mrs. B above, this man felt he got what he deserved, and was therefore not in need of any service.

Mrs. F has very few friends. Like so many elderly living within the community, she is very isolated, with a very small support system. She has a younger male acquaintance who clearly has been embezzling her funds. He cashes her monthly check, buys her a few items, but manages to end up with most of the money for himself. She does not and will not complain about this situation.

When it came to my attention, I was angry, and at first could not understand her lack of anger. She was, on the contrary, very loving toward this man, and felt that the arrangement was most agreeable. She did not want anything done; she was insistent that what was happening was fair, and to be continued. What was being voiced was depression and what was heard again (as with Mrs. B and Mr. D) was that one gets what one deserves, and that elderly people deserve very little.

The therapist's willingness to agree to a countertherapeutic arrangement that is often highly rationalized—e.g. "I don't want to stir him up"—reflects ageism on the part of the therapist. Such negotiations, when studied closely in supervision, can often be understood as a manifestation of ageism practiced together by the patient and the therapist. This can readily result in hastily done evaluations, premature decisions regarding disposition and treatment, overuse of medication, and an undervaluing of the more expressive modes of therapy.

Losses and Gains

Within a nursing home many patients isolate themselves and reject invitations to socialize and participate in milieu programs. Outreach efforts will be resisted, if not flatly refused. Pain and suffering will be hidden and denied; patients withdraw into loneliness and isolation.

Many harbor bitterness and resentment at being old, so they refuse to let anything nice happen to them. For this reason they will not let the nursing home become a "home," and behave in a style that serves to maximize their own discomfort. Some will carry this to such lengths as to cause their own expulsion from the home. Many can provoke mistreatment that they believe they deserve. More paranoid patients will assume that everyone hates them almost as much as they hate themselves. Many will more quietly and compliantly resign themselves to their fate, but put no energy (cathexis) into their situation.

Other patients enter older age having made a relatively comfortable adjustment, until a sudden loss, or even gain is experienced. A loss of a friend, spouse, pet, relative, can serve as the precipitant for a sudden decline and death. Loss of hearing or sight can result in a sudden change in a patient's mental status. A move to a new locale can be very disturbing. Loss of a job and/or retirement can, for some, be devastating. But a gain can also result in disruption. Mrs. R. illustrates this in a revealing way.

She had always functioned well, and had worked hard her whole life. Her earliest memories were of making sacrifices so that she could be helpful and available to her parents, and later to her children. Two years earlier she had retired and adjusted to this gallantly, if not with complete satisfaction. Her religion continued to play a central role in her life.

Now a widow, with grown children who were all busy in their own lives, she managed to keep active. She continued to drive, and filled her time doing volunteer work and attending a drop-in center for seniors.

At the center, she met a man with whom she began to spend time; the more they saw one another, the closer they became. Paradoxically, she became depressed and agitated. When I met her for a consultation, she was in

considerable distress. She acknowledged her loneliness. With mild resentment she stated that her children were all taken up with their own lives and
had little time for her. She said that she would like to live with one of them,
but that was out of the question. Quite suddenly she had been overcome with a
feeling that she could no longer take care of the family home where she had
lived for years, and she had decided that she must go to a nursing home. This
decision, remember, was made by a woman who until 1 month before had
done a superb job of taking care of herself and the home.

She then began to talk about her new male acquaintance. She had kept
him a secret from her children, and had trouble talking about him and how
nice it was to spend time with him. He suggested that they live together.
Although she was surprised and pleased, she was also upset. She responded
that this was out of the question, but that she would consider marriage. He
tried to explain to her that their economics were less affected if they lived
together.

She became very anxious, and consulted a parish priest, who reinforced
her guilt by telling her that it was sinful to live with a man, adding that he was
too much of a burden, and that she ought not to see him. She severed the relationship, and then decided that she must give up her house and enter a nursing
home. When reminded that her friend made her happy, she became more
upset. When asked why she felt she did not deserve some happiness in her
life, she became still more agitated.

The pleasure she gained from this new relationship precipitated a serious
crisis in her life. The pleasure made her feel as if she must choose between
being a lonely old lady, or one who deserved to have some happiness in her
life. Her guilt at the prospect of enjoying herself was so severe that she
became depressed.

The internal conflict was so intense that the easiest and least painful
remedy for the immediate problem was to abandon the relationship, and to
assuage her guilt by checking into the nursing home. Efforts at intervention,
including a consultation with a more "liberal" priest are underway, and are
being vigorously but not totally resisted. Her decision is tragic, in my opinion, because everyone loses. Her quick decision to treat her own depression
by removing herself totally from the conflictual situation substitutes symptom
relief for a slower resolution of the conflict (accomplished through a life
review and a supportive, insight-oriented therapy) which might heighten the
pain initially, but lead to a longer range solution that could result in a fuller
and richer life.

Mrs. R.'s tragedy exemplifies that of many older people who refuse
assistance. Our interventions must be designed to help our patients and clients
come to the realization that they deserve more than they allow themselves to
have. All practitioners should have at their command a range of techniques
that they can use with comfort and enthusiasm. And for any of these techni-

ques to be useful, *the goal must be to help reconnect troubled elders so they regain their self-esteem.* The creative arts may be unique in facilitating recon-nectedness—the goal of any successful intervention. They are "strong medicine" that needs to be prescribed more often.

This book defines interventions that will better equip therapists of any and all persuasions to meet the challenge of providing relevant service to a growing number of troubled elders who now often receive no service or in-adequate service. In other words, all practitioners must work toward the goal of helping people realize that cobblers and the elderly deserve an invitation to the king's court, as their presence there, or anywhere, is needed and valued.

PART I

THE DRAMA IN OUR LIVES

Drama is intrinsic to all of us as we play different roles throughout the struggle of our lives. In this section, the writers give us myriad examples of the revelatory power of theatre as art and as therapy to express feelings, disclose problems, and find solutions for them.

Naida Weisberg and Rosilyn Wilder, the co-editors of this book, are seasoned creative arts leaders/therapists when they meet their first groups of older adults. But greater demands are never put on their abilities as when they try to engage men and women who question the value of play and imagination at this stage in their lives.

Don Laffoon, Victoria Bryan, and Cynthia Cavan Sinatra of the Stop-Gap Company employ a method they call the "thera-play," which is designed to present specific issues to senior audiences for their consideration and reflection. This ensemble addresses itself to the erasure of generation stereotype. Their unique programs introduce us to many new ideas and possibilities.

Rose Pavlow, as a creative drama specialist/drama therapist, draws on years of experience to inspire enthusiastic participation and self-renewal among handicapped elderly in senior centers. She offers a range of activities and techniques that are infused with humor and playfulness. Highlighted in this article are intergenerational workshops with teenagers and preschoolers. Movement, poetry, storytelling, role play, and media are all part of her work.

Paula Gross Gray, as Director of Activities at a large metropolitan nursing home, combines her expertise in therapeutic recreation, gerontology and theatre arts to produce drama programs of quality, endorsed by administration and staff. She considers the essentials of working within the institutional system and describes a number of methods for kindling interest with both frail and alert groups.

AL WEISBERG

Rosilyn Wilder and Naida Weisberg

Naida Weisberg, M.A., Registered Drama Therapist(RDT) is a creative drama specialist. She received a B.A. in Sociology from Smith College and an M.A. in Educational Drama from Goddard College. She is a co-founder of !IMPROVISE! Inc., a nonprofit organization of creative drama specialists active in Rhode Island since 1970 a group which received the 1983 Creative Drama for Human Awareness Award from the Children's Theatre Association of America. Mrs. Weisberg is the editor of *Creative Drama News,* a nationally circulated letter/magazine and *Dramascope,* the newsletter of the National Association for Drama Therapy. Leader of training courses for activities directors in nursing homes and creative arts for older adults, she also works with teachers and children of all ages and abilities in schools and in libraries as well as with deinstitutionalized adults. Her memberships include the National Association for Drama Therapy; American Theatre Association; Advisory Board, National Educational Council of Creative Therapies; Board, Rhode Island Alliance for Arts in Education; Commissioner's Advisory Council on the Arts, RI State Department of Education; Northeastern Gerontological Society.

Rosilyn Wilder, Ed.D., Registered Drama Therapist (R.D.T.) is a drama consultant/therapist, creative arts therapist in geriatrics, and a college teacher. She is the director of *Encomium Arts Consultants, Inc.,* a placement service for artist/leaders and arts therapist teams in nursing homes, day care centers, hospitals, and colleges. She has been coordinator of *Project Vital,* a model program, partially funded through the Essex County Division on Aging, N.J., for institutionalized elderly, which includes training workshops with geriatric professionals. She also leads workshops in drama therapy, creative drama and communication in colleges, and institutions. She is an adjunct at New York University, Graduate Program in the Creative Arts, and a theatre instructor at Hunter College. She is the author of *A Space Where Anything Can Happen* (New Plays-Books, Inc., Rowayton, Connecticut, 1977.) Her memberships include the National Association for Drama Therapy, Board of Directors and editor of *Dramascope,* the national newsletter; National Educational Council of Creative Therapies, Gerontological Society of New Jersey; and the American Theatre Association. In 1981 she received the *Creative Drama for Human Awareness Award* from the Children's Theatre Association of America.

FIRST ENCOUNTERS

Naida Weisberg, R.D.T.
and Rosilyn Wilder, R.D.T.

In a Senior Center

"Who's going to pretend? Old people like us?" asked one of the senior men at the community center. He stood in the doorway for several minutes surveying the room I had just rearranged. Prior to the arrival of my first drama class with seniors, I had moved the folding chairs from their rows into a circle.

"Pretend! You mean 'make believe'? That's what kids do!" said a heavily-rouged woman. She eyed me with suspicion as she picked out a chair nearest the door.

I regretted my decision to let the senior adult director explain my program before I arrived, because creative arts processes are not easy to define; they require experiencing. And my years of working with every other age group should have warned me that elderly persons in particular would feel threatened by the words "drama", and "pretend"—a child's word, after all.

I was now facing a group of 15 elderly citizens I had never met before, who were picked up at home by the senior bus 1 to 5 days a week for the mid-day meal at the center and for the program that would occasionally follow. I was uneasy, and so were they.

After introductions, without another word I cupped my hands as though I were holding something small, fragile, and alive. I patted "it" and passed it to Louis on my right. He grinned and said that by the size of it, it was a baby bird that should still be with its mother. When he, in turn, placed the imaginary bird into Joe's hands, Joe looked at me with embarrassment. "What should I do with it?" he asked. "Anything you want," I answered gently. "Turn it into something else, something you'd like to be holding right now." As though he had played this way many times in the past, Joe inhaled the fragrance from a bouquet of flowers and presented them with a zestful flourish to the woman on his right.

The atmosphere in the room that had been filled with apprehension and discomfort now felt friendly and relaxed—even after this very brief period of time.

Then the woman whose name was Angie, unwrapped an imaginary shawl and placed it carefully around the shoulders of her neighbor. Mrs. Miller was a woman of great physical dignity but she was disoriented, and repeated herself. Now she spoke with deliberation, "This is beautiful and warm, Angie. Thank you. Do you know that I used to crochet sweaters and hats and afghans for everyone in the family, even shawls like this. They used to say I must crochet in my sleep, I was so fast." The group was astounded. They were unprepared for Mrs. Miller's clarity, for this sudden sign of wellness. And Angie, who had precipitated the response, beamed with an awareness of her own contribution.

It was apparent that the group were unaccustomed to sharing, remembering, and making connections with one another. Even after a few other playful exercises which they obviously enjoyed, they were not convinced they deserved such pleasure.

"This is what actors and actresses do, isn't it?" asked the woman in the chair nearest the door. "So why are we...we're not actors and actresses."

"Do you enjoy pretending?" I asked, trusting the process, but holding my breath just the same. "Oh yes, I do, I do," she answered. "I just can't believe that we're doing this here. It's fun. I didn't think folks like us could have such fun."

When we said our goodbyes until the next week, I found myself surrounded by friends who were eager to know about my "plans for next weeks's workshop."

At a later date, in another senior center, a wheelchair skeptic startled me by asking what the "bottom line" was in "this drama class." I had never heard the expression "bottom line"applied to drama before and stammered over my reply. I knew that if I had said "to have a good time," he would have fled the room. "Self-discovery," I suggested. "Fresh insights." "Increased perception." "Development of creative potential." His dissatisfied look did not melt. But then I had a hunch.

"What do you think of work?" I asked.

"Work is good," he said. "Work is important."

"Work gives you a reason to live," someone else chimed in. "If you don't work, you have no reason to be proud of yourself."

"How about play?" I asked. "Is it any good?"

"Oh yes, play is very important. It's good for you."

"What's so good about it?" I was beginning to feel a little bit better.

"Play is like recreation."

"Play relaxes you." Now they were all talking at once.

"You get a lift from play."

"You learn a lot from it."

"Play is work, too," from a gentleman who had not spoken before. He quickly added, "We used to be told 'no more play' when we got to school, and I don't think I've played since then!"

There was chuckling all around after this remark with everyone sharing memories of strict classrooms. Then finally came the clincher from my "bottom—line" challenger: "If you forget how to play, you forget about living!"

In an Institution

Although many long-term care facilities—including those mentioned in this book—offer fine programs for residents, many continue to be like remote caves in which there is little to do but wait. Residents sit facing large television screens seeing neither the images nor each other. There is a prevailing sense of hopelessness and remoteness from the light of the outside world. "It's a place you check into, knowing you will never check out," one resident explained to me.

I have found that the creative arts can stimulate happy participation, shared experiences, and moments of optisism even in the bleakest environments. The first time we enter a facility—you or I—can be the most difficult. But once we have experienced how our creative interventions cause eyes to brighten, or the release of unaccustomed laughter from even a few, our commitment is made.

I vividly remember the first all-day workshop I led in a state nursing home—one of the better ones, as I was to learn. In the morning I trained administrators, nurses, and other professionals. As I told them, my objective was to demonstrate how—in a group effort—drama, movement, images, words, sounds, and songs can help spark aliveness, involvement, memory, sharing, and laughter; how they can, with sensitive guidance, gradually restimulate residents' interaction and spontaneous self-expression.

After the first session, 10 non-ambulatory patient-volunteers were brought in to participate with us. I was particularly aware of one resident, a Mrs. Garnett, as an aide wheeled her through the door, erect and expressionless behind the writing tray of her wheelchair. She recoiled from the animation of the large group, mostly strangers. Her look was of someone who had been forced suddenly out into the light. She broke into sobs. A young physical therapist swiftly crossed to sit beside her, grasping her hands in his. I froze. "I can't do this!" These words sounded in my head. Yet I heard my voice begin the session; years of experience leading other age groups supported me.

I reached into my large bag-on-wheels to pull out a brightly striped, 2 inch-wide elastic sewn into a circle large enough for all to grasp. With rhythmic music on the record player, I queried, "How many ways can we move this elastic, all together?" "Up, down," contributed a nurse. "Let's row a boat," said an old gentleman. We rowed together; we pulled, stretched, waved, undulated; we breathed in unison. Faces flushed with the activity; smiles appeared.

My gaze returned to Mrs. Garnett's face. She had stopped crying; her hands still firmly clasped those of the physical therapist. Later, I saw her raise her eyes to listen solemnly as feisty Mrs. Atkinds, one hundred years old, shared a pantomine, and then described the early morning routine in the nursing home. She mimicked faces and voices of nurses and aides dashing in and out of her room. Others, professionals as well as residents, added details from their experiences.

Then Mrs. Atkinds sobered us, "Except for this hour with all of you, I'm getting dopey sitting in this place...no one to talk to. I'll forget who I am..."

By the end of that hour, everyone knew each other's names. In many facilities even this small measure of identity is overlooked. Each person had shared something of his or her life, verbally or nonverbally. A man who had been a "high-class waiter" left his walker to enact an hilarious dinner scene in which he advised three diners not to order the soup. A woman instructed us how to make a pie she had not made in 35 years-with gestures.

And then, from her wheelchair, came Mrs. Garnett's response to my question, "What does this shade of green remind you of?" She said, "A drive...a drive through the Vermont mountains...about 40 years ago." She spoke haltingly of the remembered greens of the forest reflected in the wet pavements from a summer rain. I noticed others close their eyes, the better to relish the scene.

After the residents had left, the professionals analyzed the session. One social worker labeled my approach "similar to reality therapy." And in a way it is. Also like sensitivity, remotivation, rehabilitation, and others. We all aim to stimulate individual aliveness. But note a difference: Six sessions later, the same person said, "*We* work mainly from set, prescribed activities. It seems to me the creative arts leader offers a range of choices. You listen and take cues from the participants. You aren't afraid to give them autonomy...to let them express themselves in their own ways."

As creative arts specialists and drama therapists, we do work with a play process that seems to breathe energy and spontaneity into groups of individuals, no matter what their age or problems. It evokes their gut reactions.

One reason is that this process, as the social worker observed, welcomes many different kinds of responses from the participants—which is exciting. For another, it unclouds the senses, which releases the imagination, body, and spirit.

"Children must play in order to grow up normally" most of us accept as fact. When we are young, it is the natural way to understand and express very basic feelings about our lives. As we mature and grow older, however, most of us "forget how to play," as the gentleman at the senior center signaled. We need other methods and means to recapture our powers of spontaneity and creation—so we do not "forget about living." Drama and dance, music, visual art, and writing—all of these art forms can provide outlets similar to those of play when they strengthen our capacities for self-expression. Actually, we might call them nonprescriptive "medicines," because they can heal; they can treat lethargy and depression with only the most positive side effects. Individually or in combination, the creative arts are guaranteed to induce alertness, enthusiasm, a sense of fulfillment and joy—especially when taken regularly and in large doses!

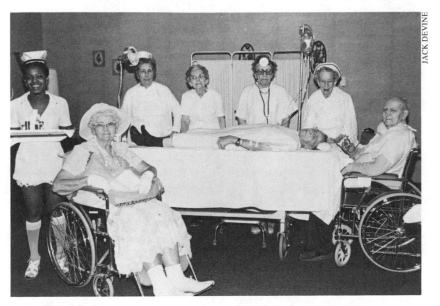

"Lordie, lordie, it's my heart." An original production by residents at the Heritage Hall Nursing Home, Agawam, Mass. Directed by Judes Ziemba.

*Resocialization is an important aspect...
learning to be with other people again despite
decreased capabilities is essential for re-entry into
society.*

Don Laffoon, M.A. Theatre; is the Co-founder and Artistic Director of California's STOP-GAP Theatre.[1] He was also the Founder and Artistic Director for 6 years of the National Children's Theatre of Iran, which toured Australia, Germany, and Jordan. Laffoon translated into English a Persian fantasy called *The Butterfly,* published by Anchorage Press.

Victoria Bryan; is the Co-founder and Executive Director of STOP-GAP Theatre. A graduate of the Royal Academy of Dramatic Arts, London, England, she has worked for the Abbey Theatre in Dublin, Ireland. Ms. Bryan has designed 21 productions for Newport Harbor Actors' Theatre in California. She is an author and filmmaker, with extensive credits in the field of educational television.

Carol Cavan Sinatra, B.A. Communication; M.S. Psychology; is a Writer and Director for childrens' theatre. Currently she is Drama Therapy Specialist for STOP-GAP.

[1]Senior Theatre Outreach Program on Growth and Aging Problems

STOP-GAP
SENIOR THEATRE OUTREACH
PROGRAM

*Don Laffoon, Victoria Bryan,
and Carol Cavan Sinatra*

Stop-Gap is a professional, nonprofit theatre company which uses creative dramatics, improvisation, performance, and what we call the "thera-play" to serve multi-generational and special needs groups.

We are seven full-time professionals whose diverse backgrounds provide experience in music, storytelling, acting, playwriting, directing, mime, design, photography, and psychology. We work as an ensemble; each member performs more than one of the functions which constitute our program.

We use theatre to build bridges of communication between generations, thereby reintegrating families and communities, and exploring the creative potential of all individuals, regardless of age, circumstance, or disability. We also use drama as a therapeutic tool to improve impaired physical, mental, emotional, and social functioning.

We find that by helping all ages understand the process of aging, we can explore the unique gifts each age has to offer. Our intergenerational philosophy is the central vitalizing force of our work, and is reflected not only in the groups we serve and in our selection of material, but in our staff itself. The ages of our staff range from twenty-four to beyond seventy; with this intergenerational composition, young and old working together as an effective unit, we feel we represent a mini-model of an ideal society.

The "Thera-play"

One of our principal techniques is called the "thera-play." A brief issue-oriented play that provides focus for a specific audience, it is designed so that one or more of the audience/participants can be involved as characters. The play is followed by a discussion during which members of the audience and the Stop-Gap company talk about the issues covered. We have found this techique to be effective with a wide range of groups, including the very frail and confused.

The thera-play works for the same reasons theatre works. It is non-threatening. It is a gentle kind of therapy. It gives the participants an opportunity to view situations similar to their own, safely and anonymously. The advantage of this is increased objectivity. Participants can consider and reflect upon what they see and hear without making definite commitments to a course of action and/or to its consequences. This, and the opportunity to identify with a character, has a liberating effect.

Touring

We always familiarize ourselves with the environment of the participants and work closely with the staff of each facility before we begin a program. Together we assess the needs of the group and then choose the techniques that will best facilitate desired results.

Through the material we use, almost all of which is original and specifically designed for whatever population we are working with, we stress that many of the problems we face are ageless. Depression, loneliness, and anxiety, for example, are problems which know no age limitations.

We arrive at the site well before performance time so we can get to know the participants and build a sense of trust. We begin the actual program by telling them who the play is about and where it takes place. Then we move into the focusing technique of board work.

Constructing the "Set"

Our artist stands at a blackboard and the participants help construct the setting for the play by telling her in detail how they think the set should look: Where does the door go? Is there a lamp? A desk? What style is it, etc.? Sometimes aphasic patients have recalled lost or forgotten speech; and stroke victims in process of regaining their speech are stimulated to practice. The group invests much of themselves by giving suggestions that reflect their own lives. Many of the men check to see that the wiring details are in order in the set. And the artist draws everything according to their instructions.

The Play

When the set is complete, the performance begins, with at least one of the audience/participants cast as a character in the play. We do not memorize lines. We hold our scripts while we perform. Typed with special large print, wide spaces, and carefully marked with each of the participant's lines underscored, the scripts are made easy to follow. This is a practice that seems to create a relaxed atmosphere. A casual read-through of the script before the program begins, to familiarize them with the material, also makes the participants feel comfortable and secure.

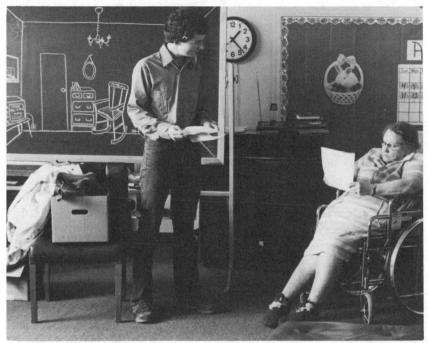

STOP-GAP actor/therapist Robert Knapp presents "script-in-hand" play with participant in a Senior Day Care Center, Garden Grove, California.

By involving one or more of the seniors as characters in the play, we obtain a commitment from them as well as from the rest of the group. The "actors" represent the others. Without this identification through one of their own members, there is the potential for the audience-members to distance themselves from us; to view us and the program as entertainment without becoming involved.

The audience members of the group give a great deal of support and encouragement to the member who has been chosen to read a part. Also, as observers of characters with problems similar to their own, the group gains a clearer perspective of the problem and its source. They see it from the involved other's point of view, perhaps for the first time. It is a good opportunity to learn effective coping skills and a time to figure out alternative solutions, perhaps never before considered. In fact, one of the most important aspects of this program is the platform it provides for older or disabled persons to speak and to be heard, a feature that is all too often lacking in their lives.

Cooperative Benefits

One group of seniors discovered that some of the difficulties they thought were specific to their own age group were indeed shared by at least one other generation. Following a play about the cost of housing or fixed income, they talked about this. A problem many seniors face today, it is also a problem for many young people. One of the seniors suggested that a solution might be found through cooperative benefits. For example, the older person could keep his or her home and open it up to a young college student, thereby sharing the cost of housing. The young person would gain a nice, homey environment, very welcome to one away from home perhaps for the first time. The older person would gain someone to help with physical maintenance and even to run to the store occasionally. And, most important, both would feel less lonely.

Following the presentation, there is always a discussion of the issues covered in the play: What was happening? How did the characters feel about the events? How would the seniors improve upon the characters' methods of dealing with the problems presented? This has been helpful not only in sharing ideas and gaining a deeper understanding of issues, but in creating group cohesion.

Network of Support

During our discussion at a senior center, several widows talked about their loneliness. They had each successfully structured their days to combat this, but at night depression overtook them. One of them suggested they tackle this problem together over dinner, conversation, and knitting, and plans were made to do just that. A real network of support began to develop outside the daytime senior center.

The participants not only draw on their personal, real-life experiences for examples and for alternative solutions to the problems presented in the play, they also offer their ideas and suggestions for future plays. We go away from the sessions feeling as though we have learned as much from the participants as they have from us.

Script Sources

Stop-Gap creates original material based on ideas from three main sources: (a) recommendations from the site directors and staff; (b) oral histories from participants; and (c) thoughts generated by our own interactions with the seniors. The staff of the host agencies frequently informs us of general areas that need to be addressed or specific problems that people are experiencing within their own lives. The most common issues are anxiety/stress, loneliness, lack of assertiveness, pain, and critical adult transitions: changing family roles, and, ultimately, dying.

Often, these issues manifest themselves in intensely possessive behavior, a problem of territorial rights, i.e., "This is *my* chair and no one else better try to sit in it!" We developed a play in which two women in a senior center argue over which one of them is sitting in the "right" seat. Performance of this play has provoked many knowing looks and nods of affirmation, indicating that a mirror held up to a common dilemma opens the door to possible solutions.

One of the most rewarding examples of a play developed from oral history has been Ed's story. Ed described himself as an aggressive, workaholic type who was always the breadwinner, and his wife "only" the homemaker. Then Ed had a disabling stroke. He was no longer able to go out and earn a living. His wife, out of necessity, took a job outside the home, and as Ed recovered from his stroke he decided to try his hand at taking over some of the housework. Much to his chagrin, homemaking was not such an easy task after all! After much trial and error, Ed grew more comfortable with his new role and now views his work with great pride. Ed has found new respect for homemaking and for his wife who has successfully crossed-over into the world of work outside the home.

Stop-Gap transformed Ed's story into a play about role-reversal and it has helped many other seniors who suddenly had to learn to perform their partner's function because of death or disability. During discussions, many seniors have expressed their happiness at being able to watch their children and/or grandchildren experience greater freedom and flexibility within marriage by sharing roles and duties with their spouses.

Our interactions with seniors frequently give rise to subject matter for plays. In one center, when we began our sessions, there was much lamenting over the shortage of men present. Most of them were playing pool. This caused the women to question their femininity and appeal "at our age." They wondered if they had lost whatever they may have once had that attracted men. Many women feared they had become boring.

In response to their plight, a Stop-Gap staff member wrote a play called *Finding a Man*. In the play, a woman in a senior center decides to follow the current media advice of trying to look and act young, to be someone other than herself. The women in the group appreciated the chance to discuss this issue and to identify some of the causes of the problem, such as mass media brain-washing. They were eager to attack prevalent myths of our culture concerning age and beauty. They shared many ideas about their own values and the uniqueness of their contributions to society. The women also pinpointed loneliness as a major problem. They discussed the value of friendship with other women, involvement in activities with people of varying ages and backgrounds, and helping others as ways to alleviate some of the loneliness, as alternatives to "finding a man."

Seniors Write Their Own Play

After a long relationship with us, one day-care center group decided to write a play of their own. They invented the characters and decided on the situation, plot, and dialogue. They drew on real-life experiences and together decided on the theme: to move or not to move to a retirement community. Their main characters were Claude and Cora Fish who were being encouraged by their daughter, Jelly, and son, Joe, to move to "Deadwood." Many seniors had friends living in such communities, or had been approached by realtors. Other characters included one of the residents of Deadwood, I. M. Shafted, and the seller of the unit there, Mr. Soap. We assisted them by taking notes and pulling it all together in the form of a finished script. The play was performed at the monthly family support night at the center. It offered everyone in the group a means for expressing original ideas, and a sense of accomplishment.

Stroke Victim Enabled

Harry was a former lawyer who had suffered a stroke and was unable to speak. Part of his normal therapy was painstakingly to write down words on index cards at home and bring them into the center the next day to use in conversation. We developed an entire play around a character who couldn't speak, but communicated by holding up flash cards. In this way, Harry was able successfully to play the part, and make a significant contribution to the whole group.

Trust

Resocialization is an important aspect of our programs. Learning to be with other people again despite decreased capabilities is essential for re-entry into society as well as reintegration into family units. Within our sessions, participants learn the value of nonverbal communication through mime and other performance techniques. Even the most hesitant participants, shy because of their diminished verbal abilities, begin to trust their fellow members and their own capacity to contribute to the group.

One very shy, hesitant woman in a senior day care center refused to do anything because she had no confidence in her ability. But one day she haltingly began to participate in the "mirror game" from her seat. The feeling of success she achieved began to grow, until at length she volunteered to be a character in a play.

Themes

Our repertoire of these short plays is extensive. Our themes include loss of independence, confinement after illness, memory, assertiveness, giving up one's home, a grandparent living with the family, nutrition, con artists, senior rights, advocacy, senior abuse, prejudice, and the economic conditions of the elderly.

In addition to individual plays, we have developed a series around a central character, Grandma, and grandson, John. Grandma and John communicate well, but they share one problem: making themselves understood to "that generation in the middle," John's parents. The Grandma character is a kind of "super senior" and serves as a positive role model. She has similar problems to those senior adults who are our target audience, and they take turns playing Grandma from week to week. Through the course of these plays, Grandma learns to cope effectively with a new living situation, learns to assert herself, gets to know her grandson and his world better.

In a Hospital

We also work with senior patients in the pulmonary dysfunction unit of a hospital. They are a sophisticated group, intellectually active, and perceptive. We have found that improvisation allows them to have control over the situation as they guide our actors through circumstances they face daily. All of the improvisations are based on situations requested by the patients. The audience/patients assume the role of "director," and the Stop-Gap actors provide a voice for them, a means of expressing their anguish and conflict.

In one instance, an actress was playing a character with pulmonary dysfunction, who was having trouble breathing. Within the improvisation, she wanted more frequent treatments from the medical staff but they refused her because it would have been detrimental to her health. A senior stopped the improvisation to tell the actress she needed to be much more panicky, and that she should pull her knees up to her chest because this would help her breathe a little easier. Then another senior, a former schoolteacher, interceded and became part of the improvisation, teaching the actress a technique for relaxation and improved breathing.

Drama as a Therapeutic Tool

Stop-Gap aims to increase public awareness of the problems of growth and aging and of mental and physical disabilities. Using drama as a therapeutic tool provides a vehicle for the expression of emotions and a means for exploring more productive ways of living. It opens the door to closer relationships and a deeper understanding between people who on the surface appear to be very different, but underneath are human beings facing the same basic issues common to us all.

SUGGESTED READINGS

Fleshman, B. & Fryrear,, J. L. *The arts in therapy*. Chicago: Nelson Hall Publishers, 1981.

Moreno, J. L. *Psychodrama*. (Vol. I) New York: Beacon House, 1946.

Moreno, J. L. *Sociodrama: A method for the analysis of social conflicts. (Psychodrama Monographs, No. 1)*. New York: Beacon House, 1944.

Slade, P. *Experiences of spontaneity*. London: Longman, 1968.

Spolin, V. *Improvisation for the theatre*. Evanston, Illinois: Northwestern University Press, 1963.

Way, B. *Development through drama*. London: Longman, 1967; UNSY: Humanities Press.

Chapter 3

REPRINTED BY PERMISSION OF THE PROVIDENCE JOURNAL-BULLETIN.

The Warwick Geriatric Day Care Center, Warwick, Rhode Island.

A partylike atmosphere had developed during the session, and when it was time to leave, they were all good friends. It was obvious to me that the teenagers and the seniors had begun to bridge the generation gap.

Rose Pavlow, M.A. Creative Drama; Registered Drama Therapist (R.D.T.); has been a Creative Drama Specialist and Drama Therapist for almost 20 years. She conducts classes for normal and handicapped of all ages in Rhode Island schools and libraries. Co-founder of !IM-PROVISE!, Inc., a nonprofit corporation of Creative Drama Specialists, Mrs. Pavlow works with elderly at senior adult centers and trains geriatric leaders in the techniques of improvisation. She is a member of the Advisory Board of the National Educational Council of Creative Therapies, National Association for Drama Therapy, and the American Theatre Association.

" . . .SECRETS I NEVER TOLD BEFORE . . . "
CREATIVE DRAMA AND DRAMA THERAPY WITH HANDICAPPED ELDERLY

Rose Pavlow, R.D.T.

Beginnings

It was really because of my mother that I considered initiating a program in creative drama with the elderly. At that point in my career, I had already been actively teaching drama to children in educational and community settings for 13 years. I believed that a similar program would be equally effective for the elderly.

My mother was quite vigorous for her age, with many outside interests, and even though she lived in a housing complex for the elderly, she was always a close, integral part of our family and friends, and an eager participant in all our activities. She frequently spoke of the loneliness of many people her own age, how tiresome some of them were, and how she hoped that she would not become "tiresome" as time went on, and repeat the same stories over and over again.

I thought about the needs of these elderly, frequently infirm or handicapped, and isolated within their own age group. I knew it was vitally important to instill in them the feeling that they were still an important part of the community, with valuable resources to share. I felt also that it would be an enlightening and fascinating experience for the young of the city to learn directly from these elders, as I will later illustrate. It would help both groups to develop an understanding of the differences which frequently alienate the young and the old from each other.

Initially, I worked as a volunteer with the elderly. We met several days in succession over a period of several weeks, which gave me the opportunity to assess interests and needs quickly. I could carry over ideas and activities from one day to the next without losing momentum and enthusiasm. The disadvantages of the usual once-a-week session, particularly with a new group, is that much of the continuity and accomplishments of the previous sessions are lost.

I recognized that a creative program for the seniors should provide a structure for sharing life experiences. Folk tales, poetry, music, and the other arts could provide the stimuli and the backdrop for unfolding the color and excitement as well as the sorrows and frustrations of their lives. They could share their stories now with an appreciative peer group and a responsive leader.

However, I was apprehensive. Would people who had spent their lives in a pattern of work and family life, suppressing the desire to "play," to be imaginative—would they come to a creative drama program? Could I help them to loosen up mentally and physically? I knew I had to respect their reluctance to let go, and I would have to give them leeway and time, and assure them that their presence was important to the group even if they did not wish actively to participate.

The Space

At this particular center there were only two spaces available, a dining room with rows of long tables, or a small, cluttered room filled with materials for arts and crafts. I chose the latter, although it barely gave us room to move. We were crowded together with two wheelchairs and six folding chairs. No one could escape or even nod off, because we were packed in so solidly. I did not want a new group scattered throughout a large area; I wanted eye-contact with everyone. I wanted to be able to reach out and touch those who were practically blind, and to repeat what others had said to those who were hard of hearing. With this arrangement, we grew close and comfortable with each other.

Tape-Recording the Scene

A tape recorder often encourages responsiveness among even the habitually withdrawn, and Connie provided a classic example of this. Sitting and mumbling to herself, she seldom talked to others. She may have been trying to contribute to the group, but no one could understand her.

At one session, the group was excited about an accident en route to the center on the senior citizen bus. I felt this was a good opportunity for an improvisation. I suggested that we re-enact the incident, with different members of the group as passengers, driver, policeman, driver of the other car, and bystanders. I recorded all of this on the tape recorder. Our policeman interrogated everyone at the scene, including Connie, who was one of the bystanders. When the tape was played back, everyone was surprised. They could hear Connie, and understand everything she said. She was delighted with herself, and after this breakthrough there was a distinct change in her attitude toward the group. She smiled, laughed, and participated in our activities more frequently.

Other Stimuli

I also found that an "instant camera" was an excellent stimulus; its revelations never fail to initiate laughter and banter.

Our improvisations were often inspired by sounds made with "junk" objects and simple instruments. One favorite sound-story was the dramatization of a day at an amusement park: barkers competing with each other, food vendors enticing customers, parents looking for lost children, and children begging for rides and goodies. The group made the hoots and roars of the spook house, and the shrieks of people on the roller coaster. They whispered endearments in the tunnel of love, and chattered happily about all the fun they were having.

My Techniques Develop

In the months following, I began a second program at another senior day care center. This is the longest program I have led, and I feel that this center provides a strong base for the consistent development of my techniques with the elderly. My own growth has evolved from searching, selecting, and trying out varied ideas for improvisations and activities to draw out and motivate the group.

In comparison with the first center, this one has a much larger working space, and there are more men in the group. During the first few sessions, the men were not as enthusiastic as the women about participating in the program, but not one walked out on me!

This center is specifically for the handicapped. There are stroke victims with speech and movement difficulties, some are nearly blind and/or deaf, and several are in wheelchairs because of other infirmities. I do not necessarily plan the programs around their handicaps. But I do tell the group they should participate as long as they are comfortable. Actually, as the sessions continue, many find themselves moving and talking far beyond their self-assessed limits without consciously being aware of the progress they are making.

Our Sparkplug: Oma

It is always helpful to have someone who is lively and spirited to animate the group. Oma (German for grandmother, which she insisted on being called) is our sparkplug. She is in her late eighties, tiny, vivacious, and speaks German interspersed with English.

Oma has severe arthritis in her knees, but she is always willing to take part. Before coming to the center, she had been very depressed, and resisted any attempts by her family to help her. Getting her out of the house and involved in the center's activities was the key to restoring her vitality. She responds spontaneously to any stimulus with a story, a song, or an old German country dance. She is often amusing, sometimes sadly nostalgic, and frequently earthy and hilarious.

For warm-ups one day, we were swinging and stretching, and Oma was reminded of playing on a swing as a child. I recorded her memories:

When I was young,
I liked to swing
    high! high! high!
And when I was high up,
I liked to look in the first
    room of the house.
I was a sneaky girl.

Everytime I went high,
I thought
    what can I do?
I turned my head
    and looked at the mill
where they make the furniture.

The feeling of the moving around;
the feeling of the jumping around;
and playing with the boys;
    more! more! more!

Then the others contributed:

When I was swinging
I wanted to swing
    as high as I could.
It was a cool feeling.

Swinging is like flying —
free as a bird.

*And sometimes you
    fall on the grass.
You don't get hurt
    when you fall;
you don't see anything.*

Music Was the Key to Gil

Gil was the youngest member of the group. His personality was the opposite of Oma's; it was difficult to get him involved in group activities. At our fifth session I put on a recording of George Gershwin's *Rhapsody in Blue* and asked the group to listen and think about how it made them feel. Did it remind them of any people or places? Were any special, past circumstances brought to mind? Gil responded with emotion, "How did you know that song was one of my favorites?" He continued, "The music has got me! Secrets I never told before—I see young people dancing; I am on stage playing my saxophone. There were changes in the spotlight from red to green, to blue and yellow!"

He had opened up and was talking about his feelings. "Secrets I never told before"—Gil said it for everyone, everyone who achieves a peak experience through the creative arts.

There is a greater frequency of death among this age group, yet I rarely heard mention of those who had died or had left for nursing homes. Just prior to one of my sessions I learned that Gil had died unexpectedly. I was extremely distressed, and wanted all of us to express and share our feelings about him, and what we had learned from him. I played his favorite melodies to help us understand him a little better. We even danced to music he loved so much. Some of the impressions each of us received from Gil, his feeling about music, what he liked or disliked, his concern for others and what he liked to do, are set down here.

Rhapsody in Blue brought back old memories for Gil when he was in the orchestra—he never forgot the people dancing. Gil must have been a pretty good musician to be able to play the *Sabre Dance*.

Maybe he was longing to be young and able like he used to be before he became sick. He liked to bring the young who had gone astray back to the fold. He mentioned a young girl he had helped out when she was sixteen years old.

He told me his dearest wish was to go to New York to see the girl he had helped out. She was married. She called him and wrote to him.

Gil liked to work with his hands—I tried to "burn him up" by telling him he did good work but not much of it. It made him laugh.

I am March!

In late March I read them "Blow March Winds Blow" from *Poems* by Minerva Maloon Simpson, a nonagenarian poet and native of Rhode Island.

Come March and sing your mad wild songs of power,
The world is list'ning but for a sweeter note,
The wasted land emerges from its slumber
And trembles at the joy from robin's throat . . .

I also read a few lines by William Shakespeare:

. . . daffodils,
That come before the swallow dare, and take
The winds of March with beauty . . .

It happened to be a day of cruel, blustery, bone-chilling winds that aggravate painful conditions, and arouse strong feelings of frustration.

I decided to assume the role of "March" to give them an antagonist against whom they could direct their anger. By taking on this role, I could guide the improvisation while defending my actions as "March." The technique of becoming the antagonist creates an atmosphere of excitement and controversy that gives the group focus. My initial problem was to convince them that I was not Rose, but actually a very aggressive character called March. I introduced myself, "I am March! You think you have it hard? What about my problems? I have to listen to all of your complaints. Speak to me and tell me why you are all complaining about me. I am a perfectly wonderful month! Why are you so impatient with me? What do you want to happen?"

Amelia: March, I think you had better get out of our way because we can't stand your winds, especially when they're strong. Stop your winds blowing which we can't stand with our aches and pains.

Doris: The winds are blowing; they shake my windows and I can't sleep at night.

Marie (to Doris): Well, can't you fix the windows? (Laughter from the group. Marie takes on the role of defending March at this point.)

Mike: I'd like to punch March. It's not any good. (Mike is a stroke victim who has difficulty with speech. It is unusual for him to offer any comments.)

Tom: March, you're a stinker! (Tom is almost always reticent. I am not sure whether his comment was motivated by the spirit of the improvisation or an effort to get back at me for drawing him into the group.)

March: Why am I a stinker?

Tom: Too many storms!

March (to Mary Agnes: She is a ninety-four year old woman with a sharp, quick wit, but she is quite deaf and I must get close to her so she can understand me.): Do you like March?

Mary Agnes: I didn't say I didn't like you. I enjoy March because you are so lively.

Laura (to Mary Agnes): What's so lively about it?

Mary Agnes (to March): You are talking all the time and giving all your energy, while some of us are only sitting here and listening.

March: How do the rest of you feel about me? Everyone who has spoken so far, except for Mary Agnes, who likes March's energy, is complaining. You told me to scram; you want to punch me, push me away, or make me blow away. I think I am a very energetic month with lots of excitement. If I didn't have strong winds, how would you fly kites; what would blow the smoke away; what would clear the air?

Gail: March, you are costing me too much money for kites. I have a fortune in kites on roofs, trees, and telephone wires. (Gail is director of the center. She is an enthusiastic participant in the activities of the group when she has some time away from her administrative duties. She enjoys the opportunity to interact with her clients).

We get into March birthdays, holidays, clothing, and the problems of bringing up children. All the personal stories are shared with zest and mutual appreciation, a most important aspect of the work. We have created a sincere family atmosphere with bonds of affection and caring.

The subject of March started out with everyone expressing their weariness with the long winter months, and loud complaints about the changeable weather. Gradually, as the result of our humorous exchanges and anecdotes, the mood changed to one of lightness and laughter. I felt it was now time to leave March and explore the promise of spring.

Building a Group Poem

I selected another one of Minerva Simpson's poems, *Springtime*. The first two lines are:

I love the glorious Spring when it is unfolding
Like an old time peddler showing his filled pack . . .

"What else do you see in the springtime peddler's pack besides what is mentioned in the poem?" I asked. These are some of the responses:

Summer underwear
Crocuses
Forsythia looks like

the shape of a small bird.
Pussywillows, like a kitten's paw.

Spring hats.
But who wears spring hats now?
My aunt had one that had a nest
with little eggs in it.

Sulphur and molasses
puts hair on your chest.
After dealing with March,
you need sulphur and molasses
to build you up.

When I typed these responses—their own group poem—and distributed them at our next meeting, they were delighted with themselves.

Dramatizing a Fable

Because of the contrasting effects of cold winds and warm sun on the elderly, Aesop's fable *The Wind and the Sun* was a natural choice for dramatic improvisation during the weeks that followed. The group portrayed characters who were affected beneficially and adversely by the wind and the sun: for example, gardeners, farmers, fishermen, housewives hanging clothes, travellers, salesmen and tourists. But before they assumed their roles, I questioned them about what they were doing, where they were going and how they were feeling at the time. They became so enthusiastically absorbed in the roles they were playing, it was obvious they were drawing from their own experiences.

Seniors and Little Ones

The seniors knew that I worked with school children; they questioned me about my experiences almost weekly. I described a number of typical sessions for them, telling them also how I deal with children who have problems, and sometimes disrupt activities.

I told them about a class of kindergarten children who were pretending to be animals living in the woods. One child, who was very bright, but aggressive and full of anger, proclaimed that he was a hunter. I visualized an abrupt end to the peaceful playing of the rest of the children, so I pointed to an imaginary sign posted on a tree and read out loud, *Hunting forbidden in this area.* I explained that this land had been set aside by the government to protect the wild animals, and it was against the law to kill any of them. The boy studied the sign as if it actually existed, and then very seriously offered to act as a guard to protect the animals. This gave him the opportunity to assert his leadership in a positive way.

The seniors were impressed with the effectiveness of creative drama on this child's social behavior. They asked if it was possible to bring a group of children to the center, which pleased me, because I had intended at some point to introduce intergenerational sessions.

I contacted the directors of several nursery schools in the area to arrange for the children's visit. They were delighted, and when I informed the seniors, they could hardly wait for their first encounter.

We Make Plans

We discussed what we would do with the youngsters. We agreed it was important to accept the children's ideas, no matter what we had originally planned for them. To establish a mood for working with the children, I asked the seniors what games they recalled from their childhood. Jacks, ring-toss, and jump rope were a few favorites, and they pretended to play them. Since most of our sessions begin with warm-up movements, these were natural activities for them.

I threw out one end of an imaginary jump rope, and an amazing thing happened. A man named Everett, who always complained about being too tired to move, got up and jumped by himself. When we gasped with surprise, he commented matter-of-factly, "Oh, I was just waiting for the right moment." He had completely forgotten about his physical problems in his excitement about this childhood game.

Pilgrims and Indians

Since the children were scheduled to visit in late November, the seniors decided to improvise "the first Thanksgiving." The week before the children were expected to join us was spent reviewing the problems and difficulties the first settlers were faced with. Many of the seniors were able to relate to this because of their experiences when they were young. They pantomined chopping wood, fishing, farming, baking bread, and hunting.

I asked them what we should do to be sure that everyone would be actively involved in the play. They suggested that the children be the Indians invited to the celebration, and the seniors, as Pilgrims, would teach the Indians how to prepare the feast.

The children had been told that they would be Indian guests at the first Thanksgiving feast. When the "Indians" arrived, I introduced them to the "Pilgrims," who were already busy miming their various tasks. The large, plain, cheerless room was transformed—it became alive with an intensity of activity. Some little hands were guided into the intricacies of kneading bread and mixing puddings. Others were vigorously chopping down trees and looking for twigs to place on the fire. One very feeble senior was showing a small Indian how to dig clams.

The Wonders of Small Children

The four-year-olds paid no attention to the seniors' handicaps. They enjoyed the individual attention, whether it came from someone in a wheelchair, or a person with limited arm movement. They even seemed to understand the ones who did not speak clearly.

After the children left, the seniors, exhilarated by the experience, chatted about the wonders of small children—so bright, attractive, and affectionate. They noted the different behaviors: the timid hide-behind-the-teacher child, and the rambunctious one looking for attention.

They anticipated a visit from the five-year-olds from the same school; but it was agreed we should wait 2 weeks to give us time to plan. They saw how important it was for them to play with ideas in advance, since familiarity with a subject increases the ability to improvise. Even though some group members have very little recall from week to week, they were caught up with the excitement of the occasion, and somehow they found a way to participate and interact in the improvisations with the children.

Cranston Senior Multi-Purpose Center, Cranston, Rhode Island.

Seniors and Teens

One day I questioned the seniors about the things they weren't supposed to do as children, to help them to realize that all the behavior of today's teenagers is not as outrageous as they assumed it to be. This discussion open-

ed a floodgate of vehement criticism by a few of them. Strong words were used to describe teenagers: self-indulgent, troublesome, violent, and lacking
respect for their elders and authority. They compared the strict rules they
remembered with the complacent, uncaring attitudes of many of today's
parents. Several of the women placed blame on working mothers.

I brought in a few lines from Carl Sandburg's poem, *The People, Yes*:

> *Why did the children*
> *Put beans in their ears*
> *When the one thing we told the children*
> *They must not do*
> *Was put beans in their ears?*

With these lines I prompted the seniors to respond with memories of what
they were not supposed to do as youngsters:

> *I wasn't supposed to buy pickles*
> *on my way to school.*
> *The first thing I did*
> *was to buy a 2-cent pickle.*

> *I wasn't supposed to go on the ice alone.*
> *There was a pond near the house.*
> *One day I went on the ice.*

> *My mother came down to the pond and said,*
> *"You come home this minute."*
> *I said "No!" She came after me.*
> *Everytime she took a step, she would*
> *go through the ice because of her weight.*
> *She got wet. I ran up to the house.*
> *That night when my father came home,*
> *I got the strap.*

> *"Don't go backwards, Annie!" grandmother said.*
> *And I walked backwards, backwards.*
> *A boy caught me. I hated the boys.*
> *I turned around and, punch! punch! punch!*
> *I ran away and tripped over a barrier.*

Coincidentally, at this time I was leading a creative drama program with
fourteen and fifteen-year-old girls in a health-science course. Part of this included role-playing based on building relationships with patients of different
ages. I felt that this was an ideal time to bring the young girls and seniors

together. This would give them the opportunity to get to know each other and, I hoped, would dispel some misconceptions and stereotypic attitudes between the two age groups. I asked the seniors if they would be interested in meeting these young people, and they were willing. I had previously discussed this with the health-science teacher, and she agreed that it would be an excellent adjunct to the program.

When I first spoke to the girls about getting together with the elderly, they were not enthusiastic. But after I described some of the humorous experiences told to me by the seniors and read some of their poetry, I could sense a change in their attitude, and a heightened interest in working with these elderly.

Each Group Plans

Only two sessions were available for meetings between the handicapped senior group and the teen girls. I wanted to give each age group the opportunity to plan some part of the encounter so they would feel more at ease and comfortable with each other. By actively participating in the planning, they would also gain a sense of responsibility for its success. Both groups were familiar with my introductory activities such as name games and warm-up movements. I found it satisfying that they both suggested similar ideas for learning about each other. Because we would become a fairly large group (about 40 people, including the staff), the time-element had to be considered carefully so that the entire first session would not consist of introductory activities. I wanted enough time left for dramatic improvisation. Above all, I had to allow for flexibility within the planned structure, depending upon what happened.

The Groups Meet!

The first joint session started with an imaginary ball-throwing game. In turn, each catcher of the ball gave his or her first name. A spark of hilarity was introduced when one of the students changed the procedure a little by saying "My name is Monique, I love money." This started everyone trying to outdo the other with exaggerated likes and dislikes, beginning with their first initial.

Then I began a movement activity using long, filmy, colorful scarves. I asked them what the scarves could do, and how many different ways they could be moved. "Floating, snapping, thumping, bouncing, swirling, bumping," came the responses. We tied the scarves together to make a huge circle and danced with them to music.

Then I wanted the students and the seniors to establish a one-to-one relationship, so they would use the scarves to work both together and against each other. My point was to stimulate changes in attitudes and emotions. When I called out, "Work against each other," there was an immediate release of strong feelings and much laughter as they tugged the scarves or twisted them around each other.

Next, I led them into reverse role-playing. I first asked them what daily annoyances were most irritating to them. A consistent gripe of many of the students was that parents and siblings interrupt their telephone conversations. This led to an improvisation in which the students became the parents, and the seniors became both the teenagers being interrupted and the pesty brothers and sisters. At first the seniors were a little hesitant, but once they assumed the roles, they acted out their parts with enthusiasm. The student/parents particularly enjoyed scolding, cajoling, and threatening the "teenagers."

The Gap is Bridged

A partylike atmosphere had developed during the session, and when it was time for the students to leave, they were all good friends. It was obvious to me that the teenagers and the seniors had begun to bridge the generation gap. Next time we could further dispel stereotypes by exploring the characters in the story of Cinderella, using the techniques of interviewing.

Exploring Cinderella

In the planning sessions before our next meeting, we discussed what feelings and opinions they had about this fairy tale. Both groups felt it was about love, magic, rags-to-riches, greed, family rivalry, and good triumphing over evil. The stereotypes were the cruel stepmother, weak father, mean and jealous stepsisters, and the beautiful and good Cinderella.

At the second joint session, various seniors and students took turns assuming the roles of the father, the stepmother, and Cinderella, while the remainder of the group questioned the characters to uncover the various facets of their personalities and the causes for their behavior. I suggested that those doing the interviewing attempt to be objective, and try not to attack the student who played the role of stepmother!

One of the seniors agreed to be Cinderella's father. I started the questioning by asking him what kind of work he did. He replied, "Milkman," which he actually was, prior to his retirement. The questions from the group showed a real interest in his work and his feelings and observations about Cinderella. When asked if he noticed the poor appearance of Cinderella, he replied that he had tried to help her, but that she was exceptional. The questions and answers continued: "In what way was she exceptional?" "She was moody." "How come you left her with a stepmother who treated her so badly?" "I thought a stepmother would be good for her. She would take care of her and she would snap out of her moodiness. I realized that Cinderella wasn't up to par and was a little backward." I thought this was a strange answer until I learned later that he had a retarded daughter.

When introducing the student who volunteered to be the stepmother, I explained to the group that she may be a different kind of stepmother than expected, and may give us a rationale for the behavior of the character she was defending. One of the seniors wanted to know why Cinderella didn't have any nice clothes and why she wasn't taken to the ball. The "stepmother" replied that she had burned her nice clothes sitting next to the fireplace. "Why did she always sit near the fireplace?" "She would think of her real mother, and sit there and cry. I tried to be nice to her, but she was always crabby to me." "Why were there always bruises on her?" "She's very clumsy and bumps into things." The teenagers questioned her at length about the bruises, because there were numerous news items at the time about child abuse.

The direct questioning stopped, and the participants became "neighbors" who took opposite sides arguing about the situation. One of the neighbors insisted that the stepmother was good to Cinderella, and spent as much time with her as she did with her own daughters. There was considerable disagreement with this opinion. Another ally of the stepmother said she noticed that Cinderella was an ungrateful child and had temper tantrums. There were also pros and cons concerning the stepsisters.

I asked the group what they thought happened to Cinderella's relationship with her stepmother and stepsisters after her marriage to the prince. Some of the answers were: "She was nice to them because she brought them to the palace to live with her." "Sure, she was nice to them! She stuck them in the dungeon." One of the seniors was quite upset with this vengeful ending because she was hoping that all would be forgiven and they would live happily ever after. She was appeased when I explained to her that we were looking for different possible endings to the story.

During my next meeting with the seniors, we reviewed our joint sessions with the students. I was pleased that they remembered individual students and many of the details of the improvisations. While they were somewhat disappointed that the joint sessions could not continue, their comments indicated great satisfaction in having had the brief opportunity to interact with the teenagers. The students expressed similar favorable reactions. It was not only a valuable learning experience, they felt, but an exciting, personal encounter. They said they could not have anticipated the active and imaginative participation of the seniors.

How Significant Is Staff Support?

The uniqueness of the center where I work is that there is regular participation by the staff in my program. Even the administrator joins in the activities whenever her duties permit. For this reason I always consider them in my choice of material, because if they find a workshop sufficiently appealing they will be more supportive of the program. Staff members also will be more inclined to adopt these techniques in their own work with elderly. After all, they are the ones who can provide and maintain a continuity of relationships and respect for individual capacities between my sessions. This was recognized by the center director who invited me to lead a number of in-service workshops that showed positive results.

The administration at this center has changed several times; many new people have joined us, and a number of the original drama group are dead. But a legacy of affection and acceptance has survived and expanded through the years. Because of this sustained flow of trust, and bonds of mutual support, I have had the confidence to experiment and try new ideas. Our group of seniors has grown; the connectedness between members of the group has strengthened; and the general understanding of the possible benefits of a program of drama for seniors is, happily, fully acknowledged.

SUGGESTED READINGS

Anderson, W. (ed.). *Therapy & the arts*. New York: Harper Colophon, 1977.

Caplow-Lindner, E., Harpaz, L., & Samberg, S. *Therapeutic dance-movement*. New York: Human Sciences Press, 1979.

Koch, K. *I never told anybody*. New York: Random House, 1977.

Maslow, A.H. *The farther reaches of human nature*. New York: The Viking Press, 1971.

Mettler, B. *Materials of dance as a creative art activity*. Tucson, Arizona: Mettler Studios, 1960.

Sandburg, C. *The complete poems of Carl Sandburg*. New York: Harcourt Brace Jovanovich, Inc., 1969.

Schattner, G. & Courtney, R. *Drama therapy* (Vols. I, II). New York: Drama Book Publishers, 1981.

Simpson, M.M. *Poems*. Virginia: Young Publications, 1968.

Thurman, A.H., & Piggins, C.A. *Drama activities for elders*: A handbook for leaders. New York: Haworth Press, Inc., 1982.

LOUIS NEMETH

Children participate with elderly in a weekly dramatic workshop to improvise a scene of *The Sound of Music*.

The more seasoned professionals at the Home doubted that I could put on a show with octogenarian performers. They pointed out that the residents couldn't see, hear, or even move very well, and if all that were not enough, they could never learn lines. But the administrator was always supportive of anything I wanted to try . . .

Paula Gray, M. S. Therapeutic Recreation; M.A. Theatre Arts; Ed. D. Gerontology; is Director of Activities, Jewish Home and Hospital for the Aged, New York City. Prior to this, she directed theatre programs in nursing homes and senior centers. Dr. Gray is the author of *Dramatics for the Elderly, A Guide for Residential Care Settings and Senior Centers,* Teacher's College Press, Columbia University, 1974. She is a member of the Senior Adult Program Committee of the American Theatre Association.

Chapter 4

"HOW WILL WE DO THE SHOW WITHOUT HER?"
DRAMATICS IN A NEW YORK CITY HOME FOR THE AGED

Paula Gross Gray

Today's nursing home residents arrive at the facility with an impressive list of physical ailments; the burden of social role loss; a recent history of social isolation and passivity; a general feeling that they cannot do much of anything anymore but sit and reflect about how much they hurt, and wait for their lives to end. Within days of admission, the activities coordinator is charged with helping them find "meaningful" uses for their leisure time. Dramatics is meaningful and fun for many of the residents I work with.

Let's Put on a Play

My own first experience directing elderly actors began when a resident came up to me and said, "You know, I'd like to put on a play. I think we could do something ourselves instead of having other people entertain us all the time!" That was 20 years ago, and he became an actor in my very first play.

I had been at the Kingsbridge House unit of the Jewish Home and Hospital for Aged only a few months. Since theatre was my speciality, I welcomed his suggestion. The more seasoned professionals at the Home doubted that I could put on a show with octogenarian performers. They pointed out that the residents could not see, hear, or even move very well, and if all that were not enough, they could never learn lines. But the administrator was always supportive of anything I wanted to try; so I set out to put on a play getting around such difficulties as hearing and ambulation problems the best way I could.

With a cast of 10 actors and actresses, the eldest of whom was eighty-eight, we put on a show we were all proud of. The script was written by a student from the American Academy of Dramatic Arts. A blind lady, who claimed to have performed with one of the legendary Barrymores, played the main role; if she was a professional, acting was entirely new to the other members of the cast. We had planned only one performance, but the Home's administrator was so impressed that he asked us to do it again, and gave as many of his staff as possible time off to see it. He believed it would give them an opportunity to see the residents in a new way.

That he was correct was brought home by a remark the X-ray technician made afterwards. Shaking my hand in appreciation, she said, "I want to thank you for letting us all see what the residents can do. You know, when they come to me, they are lying flat on a table with no make-up and no dignity. I look at them and cannot help thinking that they are barely living; but today I saw that these same people are intelligent, creative people."

Our administrator was unusual in his ability to recognize the value of dramatics. He had a natural compassion and understanding that helped us all learn to appreciate the people we worked with. For the residents, our show clearly played a part in the treatment process. They were able to ignore their pains and aches and become creative, exciting, productive people once again. Any activity that could do that for our residents was worth finding out more about.

Therefore, I have spent the years ever since in seeking new ways to help elderly men and women experience new vitality through creative activities. Each time is a new experience with new difficulties to overcome, as the residents of nursing homes become chronologically older and increasingly ill and disabled. But there is almost always a way to get around a problem, and the end result is worth the effort.

We Form a Performing Group

Central House Players was formed in 1978 when I began work as Director of Activities at the Central House unit of the Jewish Home and Hospital for Aged in New York City. The residents, whose average age is eighty-seven, are predominantly Jewish and of middle-European origin, although most are long-term citizens of the United States. The majority require skilled nursing care because they are physically frail; most require walkers, and many use wheelchairs.

Our first attempts at dramatics resulted from the interest of New York professional theatre people in developing a project for the elderly. We were contacted by a group called *Dramature* who wanted to help our residents write a script and produce it with the help of a retired script writer and a director.

My experiences had taught me that elderly actors did best when they developed the script themselves through improvisation, rather than using a script written by someone else. Our first meeting of interested residents was an informal discussion in which they talked with the professional director about their own experiences. The common theme of this discussion was life on the Lower East Side. Our residents had been children of immigrant families, and they all had colorful memories of their childhoods.

The play they finally developed was reminiscent of stories by Sholom Alecheim, the great Jewish writer. They included their favorite songs, which eliminated the need for them to learn new musical numbers. The end result was a great success, enjoyed immensely by the residents and their families, as well as senior citizen groups attending from the community.

For one man, a Mr. Mendelsohn, the recognition he received for his performance was the peak of his long life. Like many of today's elderly, he had come to the Home in a depressed condition. Unlike many of the others, he could point to little in his earlier days that had given him pride or pleasure. But then, in his late eighties, he became the star of our show. He sang several solos for the first time in his life. His voice was good, but surprisingly, his stage confidence was what earned him special applause. This made him feel like somebody for the first time.

His family was amazed. They wrote the staff a letter of thanks for what they felt we had done for him. Even more important was what he had done for others—his friends in the audience, who not only enjoyed his talent, but saw themselves vicariously in his success. Radiating an octogenarian charm as he sang, he was living proof that elderly people can try new pursuits, and perform them well.

Theatre Games

The actors in the show were encouraged by their success and wanted to continue with dramatics. So we introduced theatre games, which we assured our performers would sharpen their newly acquired acting skills.[1] Other residents joined our group who were reluctant to perform before an audience, but were willing to try improvisation without an audience.

We felt that theatre games would also provide enjoyment for the frailer residents who participated in their unit's dayroom programs. To relate to the lower functioning of frail elderly, these programs required adaptation. Because we felt that theatre games could be used on each floor, activity workers were invited to attend the Players group and learn how to use the techniques. They did not have training in dramatic techniques, although one had studied mime, two were singers, and all had appeared in school shows. They were able to pick up enough from watching the sessions to use theatre games.

Activities workers should not shy away from starting a group simply because they have not had formal theatre training. There are several books on drama for seniors included in the bibliography, and there are certainly many ways of finding a trained theatre person as leader. Many college theatre departments can recommend student directors. Almost every small town has some form of local community or religious theatre group where a director might be found. If the expert local director is too busy, perhaps there is an actor within the group who would be willing to try a new experiment working with the elderly.

We used Viola Spolin's exercises as a guide for theatre games.[2] I found that we needed to adapt, or to eliminate some games, because of the physical and sensory deficits of the participants, and their initial feelings of reticence. We began with *Play Ball*, a traditional ice-breaker, using pantomime and a sharing of names. The Players responded immediately with imagination. However, our on-floor groups needed more than explanations, and it was necessary to demonstrate what we wanted from them. This may be due to hearing loss, but also to some extent to decreased cognitive capacity.

Even with the Players, as exercises became more difficult, it was often necessary to do a two-person demonstration with staff. As Kozelka suggests, the leader "must be flexible enough to teach by direct imitation, to serve as a model if necessary."[3] One particularly difficult transition occurred when we moved from pantomime to dialogue. It was necessary to remind the participants "You can talk now" several times before they began to speak.

One morning several participants arrived very disturbed about matters that had occurred on their floors. They were totally unable to concentrate on anything else. We immediately applied a relaxation exercise learned in a Behavior Modification training program presented by New York City Community College.[4] The exercise includes the development of a "calm scene." Residents do deep breathing as they describe places where they feel relaxed in terms of what they see, hear, smell, taste, and feel. On that difficult day this exercise helped. It enabled residents to forget their pain, and problems experienced before coming to our group. For many of our residents a ride on the elevator and down the corridor may be taxing.

Body movement exercises are a regular part of most of our theatre games sessions. Most of the members of our Players group have been attending a "Stay Healthy" group conducted by Sonya Samberg, co-author of *Therapeutic Dance Movement*.[5] They are able to lead each other in exercises described in that excellent volume. It is not necessary for me to teach them movement exercises. They teach me.

Expressing Feelings

When the residents improvise the expression of basic emotions, anger is one they avoid. One of the most effective ways to get a strong response from the residents I have worked with is to ask a question which forces the issue. Accordingly, when I ask, "What makes a resident angriest?" the answer is unanimous. "The food!" and is always spoken with anger.

I then suggest a situation in which a resident complains to an aide who serves him unacceptable food. The aide calls in the dietician to handle the situation. This scene always succeeds in getting our actors to let loose plenty of anger; but since they must play the aide and dietician roles as well, it also gives them insight into other points of view, i.e., how the aide may feel caught in the middle between the angry resident and a dietician who is the person with the power to do what is needed. When residents assume the dietician role, they give answers to the angry resident that show they really do understand why problems with food sometimes occur. Actor/dieticians are also instructed not to get angry at the residents, no matter what they say, and that provides some insights too. Situations indigenous to the group are profitable, although I would certainly not suggest their exclusive use. Any situation that is age-appropriate works well. Some good suggestions can be found in *Creative Drama for Senior Adults* by Isabel Burger.[6]

A Demonstration TV Show

At a conference of geriatric professionals, a colleague of mine, who was a leader of creative dramatics with seniors, asked if our group could work with her on a TV show for a special demonstration. I was confident of the skills of three of the residents who had been in our earlier production, so I agreed, stipulating that the leader must come to the Home to practice with the group before the telecast.

I need not have feared. At the first practice session the leader set characters, and our three were off on a 40 minute improvisation that had plot, characters, and even a beginning, middle, and end. One of the three in particular, Mrs. Klein, was responsible for keeping the plot moving. She was always ready to break in (in character) when the others got off the track, or to bring in the third actor when she sensed that only two of the three were truly involved. When a point had been made, it was she who introduced new elements, and the others followed her lead.

Their new leader was duly impressed. They knew it and were pleased with themselves. When told that the purpose was to do a demonstation of creative dramatics for people of their age group, they were confident they could do it and were excited about being on television.

At the next meeting the group came back with new ideas for the original improvisation. The guest leader then made it clear that the TV demonstration would consist only of fresh material, and the intent of these pre-sessions was to get them used to their new leader and her techniques. There was a little resistance to this idea, but when the guest leader and I insisted that we knew their spontaneous improvisations would be good, they reluctantly began a new plot. As they left that day, each in his or her own way let us know that they would prefer to do a rehearsed scene on TV. But we stood firm.

The last session went well. They were now reconciled to doing only fresh material and had developed a good relationship with the guest leader. We scheduled a final session for the day before the TV taping for 1 p.m.

At 12 noon on the day of the last rehearsal, one of the activities staff came to my office and said, "I think you had better sit down." She went on quickly, "Mrs. Klein has just died."At first there was my own shock—how could this be? I saw her yesterday—but yes, she did say she was not feeling well and hoped she would feel better by the day of the TV show—*The TV Show* that was to rehearse in one hour! The TV show! What will we do? Worse—how will we tell the other two residents? It was quickly decided that would have to be done at 1 p.m. when they came to rehearsal.

The hour that followed was a confusion of explanations to the guest leader who arrived minutes later and phone calls to the producer. We all felt that we had to come up with something in case the residents did not want to do the show. I told the others it was likely they *might* still want to do it. However, with our best ensemble actor gone, it might be advisable for me to be on the show as well.

Telling the Others

It was decided that the activities worker and I would tell the residents. If the new leader were present they might feel compelled to do the show. We knew from past experience that our residents would be better able to handle the announcement of such a death than we ourselves. Elderly people are more able to accept this news as a fact of life. But this case was different from most deaths in the Home in that it was a person seen as "healthy" and "involved" and not expected to die. Even within the Home most deaths occur after a noticable downward health trend and a withdrawal from activity and social relationships.

Mrs. Klein was one of the best known and active figures in the Home, and though she was wheelchair-bound, she was seen as healthy and even young. The idea that she was "young" was a notion she chose not to deny. She simply refused to supply her age. She smiled in triumph when the inevitable guess by the questioner was at least 20 years less than her actual eighty-five years. The death of someone like Mrs. Klein would be more threatening than most for our residents, particularly for the actor and actress who had worked so closely with her. Mr. Mendelsohn had a very close relationship with Mrs. Klein. We had observed that each bolstered the spirits of the other when he or she was feeling down. With Mrs. Cohen, the third member, there had been perhaps a shade of rivalry mixed with mutual respect and friendship. Both these relationships gave us reason to be concerned about their reactions to the death.

We met at our usual time and place. Feeling that it was best to let the others know right away, we simply stated that Mrs. Klein would not be coming because she had died suddenly only moments earlier. After the brief announcement we stopped talking and listened.

Following the initial shock, and questions to confirm when and how, both expressed kind and loving thoughts about their friend and how greatly she would be missed. Then Mr. Mendelsohn asked, "How will we do the show without her?" We asked if they wanted to do it. Both immediately said they would. I asked if they would feel more comfortable if I joined them; they agreed this would help. Then we held a regular session with the guest leader joining us.

But the Show Goes On

The next morning when the three of us got into the car to drive to the television studio, tension was evident. All of my attempts to make conversation fell on deaf ears. Finally I concentrated on my own fears. Perhaps for once I had expected too much of these wonderful, but after all, very old people.

At the studio entrance came another blow. We were told we were early and must wait before being admitted to the studio. The lobby was chilly and the seats were not designed for old people. Mrs. Cohen and Mr. Mendelsohn made the best of it and sat on the edge of their vinyl covered seats telling me that they were "just fine," in voices that belied their words. Again I tried conversation but my usually garrulous two were lost in their own thoughts.

In an effort to keep my actors warm I suggested that we do movement exercises. Habit triumphed. Mrs. Cohen quickly became our leader in the exercises she had enjoyed doing for so many years. Mr. Mendelsohn, on the other hand, was just going through the motions. It was clear his mind was on other matters. How could I get his attention! I suggested a relaxation exercise since Mr. Mendelsohn was very proud of his "calm scene."

Just as my actor and actress were beginning to concentrate, the cast of one of the soap operas bustled into the lobby talking exuberantly to each other. Since I don't get much chance to watch "the soaps," the residents identified the celebrities to me. Clearly it made them feel like real professionals to see these stars, whom they watched daily on TV, coming out of the studio where they themselves would soon be taped. They were ready to perform, and even the somewhat difficult experience of climbing over the cables and scenery, the make-up, and the hot and glaring lights did not dampen their revived spirits. Their improvisations and interviews were sparkling and energetic.

Mrs. Cohen led us in the same warm-up exercises she had done in the lobby, the camera picking up her shining, confident face as she did so. Mr. Mendelsohn sold us some sweaters in an improvisation suggested by the guest leader who knew he had been a salesman. We all shared an improvisation in which an imaginary baby was brought by his mother (myself) to visit his aunt (the guest leader) and his grandparents. Asked by the show's host how he became interested in dramatics, Mr. Mendelsohn told his own story in a way I would not have done, although I played a major role in it. He said it started when I had asked him to sit in the front row of an audience and chat with Robert Merrill who was taping a TV spot for charity at our Home. Mr. Mendelsohn said that my confidence in his ability to respond to Mr. Merrill built up his own self-esteem and made him willing to try the show later on. Any leader of seniors will quickly find that seniors need constant reassurance from you—"I know you can do it."

Recruiting Residents

Mr. Mendelsohn had been recruited to our group easily, but other residents were not so easily persuaded to try performing. One of my most difficult campaigns took almost 2 years. The story of my pursuit of Mrs. Weiss began when I heard this young-looking and pretty woman at a sing-along. (I have long made it a practice to lurk about during this activity, looking for likely talent for my drama group.) When we did our first show, she had been invited to join; but I was told with a wistful smile and a trace of a tear that she was not in the mood because she had not recovered from the death of her beloved husband who had died in the Home of a heart condition. Thinking that this had happened recently I sympathized profusely with her loss. I understood she might not feel like participating.

When I inquired about her on her floor I was told that her husband had died several years before, and it was about time she stopped moaning about him and put the creative talent and excellent mental faculties that she possessed to better use. This spurred my interest even more for the "perpetual widow syndrome" has always offended my no-nonsense New England sensibilities. I knew then that I had to get Mrs. Weiss to use her talents and find pleasure in her own life.

She refused, adamantly, to have anything to do with performing, but when the theatre games group began, she came. To no one's surprise, she was one of the most talented in the group. She obviously enjoyed herself thoroughly. When asked to participate in the television show she had again refused to perform before an audience, clearly feeling that she was not good enough. She dropped out of the group entirely, but returned after the show was over for our workshops.

Building a Holiday Play

At one of our theatre games sessions I asked the group if they would like to do a short skit for the Jewish holiday of Purim (a play is a traditional part of the celebration of that holiday). All agreed and were delighted to have an opportunity to perform once again. Mrs. Weiss said immediately that she would leave the group until the show was over. The others told her they would miss her, that they knew she was very good and enjoyed acting. I pointed out that one member of the cast was often absent; so would she continue with us as we developed the skit through improvisation and take the roles of absent members. She agreed to this with the caveat that she should not be expected to perform.

We began our preparation for the skit by reading the story of Esther from the Megillah. Then, as a first try, we picked two moments to improvise, allowing all participants to try whatever roles they wished. The story begins when King Ahasuerus, the King of Persia, executes Vashti, his wife of many years, for refusing to dance at a banquet. We decided that it would be fun to place the story in modern times and change the characters to people the residents could relate to.

The king became Mr. Ash, a wealthy businessman who asks his wife, a very proper society matron, to do the dance of the seven veils at a party he is giving for some wealthy clients. His wife is outraged at this request and decides to walk out on her husband and get a divorce rather than sticking around to be beheaded as she was in the biblical account. Mr. Mendelsohn took the role of Mr. Ash. He was very persuasive, then hurt and indignant at his wife's refusal to dance the dance of the seven veils at his business party. Mrs. Cohen in the role of Mrs. Ash, turned him down and walked out.

I felt the performance was not quite strong enough. I asked Mrs. Weiss to try the role. Mr. Mendelsohn once again made his request. Mrs. Weiss' first response was a mild "Why, what would our children say if I did a dance like that?" Mr. Mendeloshn came back with, "Why, they would understand, as you should too, if you were a good wife. After all, my business puts our bread and butter on the table." Mrs. Weiss looked at him and said meekly, "All right, I'll do the dance." The group and I cried out as one, "No! You can't do that. You can't change the story. You have to stand up to him and say no!" "I can't do that," said Mrs. Weiss.

I insisted that she try again and after three tries, with a lot of coaching on my part, we finally managed a limp refusal from her, which was nonetheless greeted with cheers from all of us. We tried the scene again and this time the refusal was decisive and self-assured. We went on to try some other scenes before ending the session.

After the session I found Mrs. Weiss in the hall and congratulated her on her performance, but to my distres she raised a mournful and tearful face to me. "I'm crying, and I don't know why!" she said. I suggested "Maybe, like the character in the play, you are angry about something and can't say it."

I thought about what had happened later on and realized that, in the scene, I had asked her to be angry at a man who was her husband, and to refuse his absurd demands. Staff had told me that her own husband, in his illness, had been very demanding and at times irascible. She had remained the dutiful wife, making allowances for his pain and trying to comply with all his requests. Many times she may have wanted to turn on him in anger as we had made her do in the scene, but she had never done so. She always spoke of her husband in the most glowing terms, never admitting that his last days had been difficult for all who came in contact with him, particularly herself. I felt that doing this scene might have therapeutic benefits in helping to release her pent-up anger.

Mrs. Weiss rehearsed the scene many times, but only because she was assured that Mrs. Cohen would do the performances. Unfortunately, Mrs. Cohen caught a cold in the last weeks of rehearsal and eventually developed pneumonia. During the last week Mrs. Weiss played the role at all the rehearsals. On the morning of the final dress rehearsal, Mrs. Cohen was admitted to the hospital.

I had not dared to suggest to Mrs. Weiss that she would have to do the performance. Expecting strong resistance, I steeled myself and went to speak to her. "You know Mrs. Cohen has been taken to the hospital. We really need you to play the part." Mrs. Weiss looked up and said, "I know. I'll do it."

It took a few moments for me to recover from the shock; but I still had one more request to make. Mrs. Cohen was our resident singer, and she had planned to sing a song. When Mrs. Weiss played the role she never rehearsed the song although she had a sweet voice. "Mrs. Cohen was going to sing, you know," I said. "But I don't know the song," she answered. "Do you know *Let Me Call You Sweetheart?*" I asked. "Well, of course," she said. "Good. Sing that," I said. At that point Mr. Mendelsohn entered. I told him the news, that Mrs. Weiss was going to play his wife. Before there was time for her to change her mind, I got them both on stage where they sang the song that was to open our show with a bang.

Why Improvisation?

As in all our productions, we try to fit the role to the actor rather than typecasting an actor into a role. We also try to take into account an individual's disabilities. This is one reason we usually develop our own scripts through improvisation.

To illustrate, Mr. Schwarz had appeared as narrator for our first show. He was the long-time leader of the resident council, a capable public speaker with a good loud voice—a great asset, since the majority of those in our audiences are hard of hearing. As a narrator he was praised for his strong voice.

With many male roles in the Purim story, we had to design a role for him that would emphasize his speaking ability. We also had to cast the role of the villain Haman, the persecutor of the Jewish people—a role that none of my actors wanted to play.

Mr. Schwarz had run his own business in the past; he had been on the management side in handling labor problems. For this reason, the group decided he should play Haman. Haman would be the management consultant to the businessman, Mr. Ash. He would tell Mr. Ash to make his Jewish employees work on the High Holidays. The union leader, Mordecai, would enlist the aid of his neice, Esther, to persuade Mr. Ash to fire the consultant and return to his former practices. Thus we changed the biblical story into situations our residents could relate to.

In the role of the management consultant, Mr. Schwarz came alive; he argued with great conviction the side of management versus labor. He drew upon his lifetime of experience and was acknowledged for it, even while playing a villainous role.

Integrating Children into the Drama Group

We have long been aware that one way to make our residents' faces shine with happiness is to bring small children into the Home. We have had many programs involving children: a four year-old class that visited weekly; a kindergarten and nursery group that came to help residents celebrate the Jewish holidays by singing songs and telling the traditional stories; a group of children who had difficulty reading in public school and were tutored by the residents; and many young entertainers of all descriptions. We had never had a child in any of our productions.

LOUIS NEMETH

The Jewish Home and Hospital for the Aged, New York, New York.

When the residents decided to do *The Sound of Music* and the script call-ed for children, we knew immediately that the residents and children would both gain from the experience. What happened during the year the two groups worked together was even more exciting than we anticipated. Although I have long advocated this kind of intergenerational dramatics, I now feel that children should be made a permanent part of any program.

One benefit of bringing the two groups together was noticeable on the first day. We usually met at 2 o'clock. Since the children were released from their school several blocks away at that time, they did not arrive for 20 or 30 minutes. I wanted the residents to perform at their best when they first work-ed with the children, so we spent that extra time doing theatre games I intend-ed to use later for getting acquainted.

We had not met for several months, and activities were moving along rather ponderously when the door opened and five bundles of energy burst in upon us. The residents looked up and instantly each seemed to shed at least a decade. We repeated the theatre games all together; now they rose to meet the children's youthful enthusiasm.

Both children and residents were anxious to begin work on *The Sound of Music,* and yielding to their requests, I let them try an improvisation of the first meeting of the children and their new governess, Maria. Mrs. Cohen, as the governess, sat on the sofa with the children in a circle at her feet and began to ask them questions. I told the children that they could answer as themselves. If the real Maria and her children experienced the same kind of magic as we did watching that scene, they were lucky indeed. From the first moment, Mrs. Cohen became their friend and teacher and helped all of us know them better.

As the work on the production progressed, I as director learned that there were great practical advantages to having the children on stage to assist the residents in walking and standing, since all of our group needed walkers. It was also helpful to know that when a resident missed a line, the children could be trained to feed the line to the elderly actor.

The children learned a lifetime's worth of information about aging and disability. They learned how to speak to the hearing-impaired and how they use one sense to compensate for another, impaired faculty. Most of all, they learned valuable lessons such as "even if you have one leg that isn't real, you can still go on walking and performing, and *smiling!*" Proof that these lessons were being learned came one day when I used the word "stereotyped" and the children asked what it meant. "Well," I said, "one example of a stereotype might be *all* old people are cranky and impatient with children." I did not get further. "Oh, no," they protested, "that's not true. We know better! Old peo-ple are kind and very patient. They love children!"

Whether they learned the lesson of the fallibility of stereotypes in general I cannot be sure; but I do know for certain that none of our young actors will ever subscribe to negative stereotypes of old people. Perhaps this knowledge will help them to face their own eventual aging and disability with less fear.

Where I Work

It must be acknowledged that the Jewish Home and Hospital for Aged is a very special place. The residents have a keen interest in the arts. If they have not participated before, at least they have attended as theatre-goers, museum members and concert and opera lovers. They have taken advantage over their long lifetimes of New York City's rich cultural opportunities. The Home itself, one of the oldest and largest in the United States, has a reputation for innovative programming of all kinds. In 1937, the year I was born, the residents put on two full scale musical productions of *The Mikado* and *Floradora Girls* that were reported in the *Herald Tribune* of the day. When I began my drama group in 1963, I was simply carrying on a long tradition. Accounts of productions at the Home can be found as long ago as 1922 and there is no reason to believe that there were not others before them.

Advice to New Drama Leaders

In spite of this rich heritage, Jewish Home and Hospital for Aged shares some basic realities in common with the small nursing home:

> Few of today's elderly will have had any experience actually performing and will need to be coaxed to try. The theatre games approach is a less threatening way to start for some, but there are others who will only be motivated to risk trying through the promised reward of a performance.

> There is no question that a nursing home is primarily a health care setting and therefore certain treatment schedules must be worked around; i.e., if the podiatrist or dentist visits once a week you cannot expect a resident in need of their services to attend a theatre games group instead. Other schedules, such as that of a physical therapy department in settings where it operates 5 days a week, may be adjusted with prior notice from the activities coordinator.

> If the leader is coming from the outside, he or she will need to sell the value of the program to the staff in terms of its part in the overall treatment goals of the setting. As the program progresses, most staff will pick up on the improved quality in resident morale and even in mental health. It would certainly be helpful to let nurses and aides see for themselves how participation can help residents. My administrator in 1963 knew this when he urged me to put on our show for the staff.

Even if, in some places, the drama leader is first met with snickers or open hostility by the staff, he or she must remain polite, and not defensive, if he or she is to achieve a successful program.

In all this a supportive activity coordinator can offer guidance and assistance in dealing with the internal system.

I have related these experiences with the Central House Players because I feel that they are illustrative of principles that will assist leaders of drama with the elderly. I have set forth other suggestions in my own book, *Dramatics for the Elderly,* but let me summarize some ideas implied by the material in this chapter.[7]

Dramatics has great value for the elderly actor.

It makes the participant feel successful and important;

It provides an opportunity to do something for others by presenting shows and skits;

It provides an opportunity for participants to learn to work together;

It provides an outlet for emotions.

Scripts are best developed through improvisation and built around situations familiar in some way to the participants. This allows opportunities to adapt for disabilities and personal characteristics of the actors and is an aid to memory problems.

Theatre games are a valuable activity for many residents who will not perform. Movement, sensory, breathing, and voice exercises as well as pantomine and improvisation are popular, but expanded verbal instruction and demonstration may be necessary, particularly with frailer groups.

Persons working with elderly groups must be ready to deal with sudden illness and death as facts of life.

Having alternates for roles as suggested by Robinson is helpful when possible.[8]

Working with the elderly in dramatics is a continuing challenge to the leader's or producing-director's creativity. In our last production, a parody of

Oklahoma, Curley entered with a cardboard horse attached to the side of his walker, so it appeared he was leading the horse. This provided a visual and comic treat for the audience as well as needed support for the actor.

There is no end to challenges like these in theatre for seniors and no end to the rich experience on which the elderly can draw for material. For those of us who are lucky enough to work with older people, there is much to be learned, and so many rewards.

NOTES

[1]Spolin, V. *Improvisation for the theatre.* Chicago: Northwestern University Press, 1963.

[2]*ibid.*

[3]Kozelka, P., Getting Started. *In Senior adult theatre, The American Theatre Association handbook.* R. Cornish, C. Kase (eds.) (Pennsylvania: The Pennsylvania State University Press, 1981, p. 12.

[4]Cheek, F.E., *Behavior modification training program in self-control.* New Jersey: New Jersey Neuro-Psychiatric Institute, 1975.

[5]Caplow-Lindner, E., Harpaz, L. & Samberg, S., *Therapeutic dance-movement, expressive activities for older adults.* New York: Human Sciences Press, 1979.

[6]Burger, E., *Creative drama for senior adults.* Connecticut: Morehouse-Barlow Co., Inc., 1980.

[7]Gray. P.G., *Dramatics for the elderly, a guide for residential care settings and senior centers.* New York: College Press, 1974.

[8]Robinson, H.W., *Senior adults in play production, Senior adult theatre,* In R. Cornish and C. R. Kase (eds.) *The American Theatre Association handbook.* Pennsylvania: The Pennsylvania State University Press, 1981, p. 20.

PART II

MUSIC AND SOUND
TO LIBERATE
THE INDIVIDUAL

Music is an abstract universal language that can penetrate to the human heart and spirit in an instant. It requires no introduction or bridge; aspects of harmony are part of each person's experience.

Delight Immonen, employed to lead music activities in nursing homes and senior centers, details how music can be an antidote to lethargy and disconnection. Offered sensitively, it can be a potent change agent. As a leader, she encourages initiative and personal expressions. Through choice anecdotes, she reveals how she sets goals, plans programs and adapts to each person's realities while stimulating her group members to share together in rhythm and song.

Marian Palmer delineates with discernment the planning processes of the music therapist in developing a treatment plan to meet each client's total needs. Working with group as well as individual clients, she also adapts many adjunctive techniques derived from dance/movement, reality orientation, and songwriting to promote physical, mental, and psychosocial well-being.

JOHN ISAAC

"We really should sing it for someone else..." Music at the Jewish Home and Hospital for Aged in New York City.

> *One role of a leader of a music group in a nursing home which should never be overlooked, is a sensitivity toward change potential in the various individuals present.*

Delight Lewis Immonen, Registered Music Therapist; has a B.A. in Music Education with High Distinction from the University of Michigan and a M. Music Education from the New England Conservatory of Music with a concentration in Music Therapy. She did an internship at the Boston State Hospital. For the last several years, Mrs. Immonen has been leading workshops for elderly in nursing homes and senior centers. A professional musician, Mrs. Immonen plays the oboe and English horn. She performs with the Rhode Island Philharmonic, New Music Ensemble, and The Henschel Ensemble. She is a member of Phi Beta Kappa.

"...WE'VE NO LESS DAYS..."
MUSIC AS ACTIVITY IN NURSING HOME AND SENIOR CENTER

Delight Lewis Immonen, RMT

The last verse of the hymn *Amazing Grace* closes with the words "We've no less days/To sing God's praise/Than when we first begun." In working with music and older people, I am constantly aware of this. Singing, in whatever style, with whatever instrument, provides a short space of timelessness; and most of the participants do have "all the time in the world."

In both nursing homes and senior citizen centers, *Amazing Grace* has been enjoyed: sung unaccompanied with a resident on a ward of very withdrawn patients; used as a background for instrumental improvisation on another ward in the same building; or prepared in three-part harmony with a choral group of senior citizens in a community center. The lyrics communicate a positive attitude toward music, and the simple melody reinforces this.

In this article, I will discuss various music activities in nursing homes, and others more applicable to senior citizen centers. In both settings, an activity or recreation director is the one who usually arranges for a music specialist to supplement the weekly programs.

Although I am a music therapist, I was hired as a musician to lead music activities in nursing homes and senior centers by the Rhode Island State Council on the Arts. I have worked mainly with groups rather than on a one-to-one basis, but there are many times that I am aware of the therapeutic implications of my work as it affects individuals.

Potential for Change

The potential for change in the various individuals present in a group should never be overlooked. The leader must always be on the lookout for possibilities of a change for the better, for those individuals who still have an interest in "moving." People who initiate a change relationship themselves may indicate their readiness by asking for help with a song, or for specific music at the next meeting. Or they may express a desire to learn to read music. All these requests may be met successfully; certainly they merit the extra time spent arranging music or rewriting it on larger manuscript paper if necessary.

But there may also be an unspoken, implied need for change on a deeper level—the individual asking for help to make adjustments, through music, in dealing with his or her life situation. In these instances, it is very important not to assume the role of therapist unless one is properly qualified.

Even more important, the musician/therapist must be there often enough, and over a long enough period of time, to be able to see the client, which the individual will become, through any sort of change that might be initiated. Music therapy is an adjunctive therapy and should be administered as part of a therapeutic team effort on behalf of the client. Often, more harm than good may come unless it is treated as such.

In the Nursing Home

In nursing homes, groups are generally made up of those residents who would like to "go to music," especially those who have had a previous interest in music and are urged to continue it. Many look upon the sessions as a class, and regard the group leader as a teacher. Held at the same time each week, classes are preferably announced on a calendar ahead of time. In the larger institutions, the workshops are announced beforehand over a loudspeaker.

The residents who come together for music are frequently as much strangers to each other as they are to an outsider, so it is very important that names be used. It is often a fine idea in the beginning to sing songs like "Mary," or "Sweet Sue," but substitute the names of everyone in the group. Using a song sheet that includes all the names of the members is also a good way to break the ice.

The Leader's Role

The leader of a group is, of course, fundamental to the direction a group will take. Consequently, a little soul-searching about one's own desires and expectations is important. The group leader who asks for loud singing may get just that—and only that. And the leader who likes particular songs may fashion a session to include these alone, falsely assuming the residents like them also. When group participation is truly welcomed and new material constantly elicited from the members, activities express the growth of individuals and of the group. The leader needs to take stock of the autonomy he or she wishes the group to assume.

Resistance

One form of resistance from residents often encountered by a group leader is the attitude, "Whatever you want to do is fine." Residents are used to abdicating their power to make decisions, to think, and to have opinions. A way to challenge this passivity and resignation is to ask a specific person, e.g. "Bill, would you like the group to start with 'God Bless America' or 'The Battle Hymn of the Republic'?"

Frequently I hear "I never could learn to read music . . . or play the piano . . . or sing." I answer cheerfully, "Now is now;" and follow with an activity that allows for instant success. For example, it is the rare person who says, "I always wished to play the piano," and who comes to the piano to try. But a small, moveable, keyboard instrument, brought *to* the person to play, is a nonthreatening guarantee of involvement.

Too often there is interaction between the leader and the various members of a group, but very little among the members themselves. It may even seem that the leader is initiating all activity, and that the residents are not even reacting to the leader, let alone each other. One completely nonverbal stimulus is to offer a tambourine or drum to an individual. This can elicit a musical response from the group who may sing or play as an echo to the drummer's beat.

Any group's membership, in one way or another, is composed of those whose musical expectations are either vague, based on former musical experiences, or completely dependent on the leader. In any event, all the members hope to enjoy themselves, or they would not have come—although there are times when the staff may make that decision for them.

Dealing with differences in a group's choice of material is always a difficult part of a leader's job. Perhaps it is best handled by being certain that all requests are treated with respect, even though the choices of some members may seem silly or even insulting to the others. The more capable leader will usually rise to the challenge of accepting a request for a child's song like *Three Blind Mice* by adding an extra part such as a descant to satisfy the more sophisticated members. (A descant is a counter melody; many satisfying descants are contained in music textbooks from the fifth grade on up).

Almost all requests can be filled. It is important for the leader to make everyone feel welcome by honoring his or her suggestions. It is far better, when confronted with an unfamiliar request, to say "Let me see if I can have that for the next time," than "I don't know that one."

It is not a good idea to limit choices by offering one particular set of song sheets. Group members themselves may be able to make up the words to songs, perhaps to melodies they have composed. When this occurs, their names should appear on the copies and someone with an artistic flair may design covers for the compositions.

Once material has been selected and a group established, more questions can be raised by the leader regarding:

Tempo — should that song be slower or faster?
Meter — should we play with a one-two or one-two-three beat?
Dynamics — are there any parts of that song that should be sung very quietly?

Often the most sensitive reactions may not be verbalized, and it is up to the leader to recognize this input as well. One should be aware of such cues as hand gestures and toe-tappings. In turn, the leader's responsive smiles and nods when a tempo feels correct are signs of approval and support. This acknowledgment will please the members.

Involving Guests

Meetings are generally scheduled after medications have been handed out, or before and after meals. Visitors who arrive at those times certainly wish to speak with the person they have come to see. Involving them in the informal music group with that resident will help them feel welcome and at ease. Some may even offer to play the piano, or sing, or help hand out instruments. Singing songs that visitors suggest can extend the musical experiences. This is more positive than having them talk on the sidelines. It is also a pleasant change for the residents to have their guests participate, perhaps more fun for both sides than trying to hold conversations about situations from which the resident is now removed.

Listening to Records

Recorded music can also be well received, if the record player is of acceptable quality. But one should never play endless "soothing" music at the residents. They should be allowed to discuss the selections they are going to hear and evaluate them afterwards. Their views are welcomed; they are an important part of the planning of future meetings. Listening becomes active when appropriate instruments are added or when participants tap their fingers and feet. However, the fact that a person is quiet and actually listening is not the same as "nodding off." Silence in a listening group can be the best indication of involvement.

Peak Experience

A peak experience is a special moment that will be remembered. It is often worth repeating a particular number enjoyed by all. By noticing a song which went well and suggesting that the group sing it again at the close of the meeting, one can reinforce the group's sharing. I always aim for at least one peak experience during a session, in case a member is not present at future meetings. Each session should offer a complete experience in case some of the long-term musical goals prove to be impossible. These long-range goals should never be ignored, however; and discussions with the staff of the institution will help to relate them to the goals of other planned activities for the members.

You Can Do It

Attempting to teach someone something implies that that person is worth the time spent, and the teacher judges that person capable of learning; so even if some members of the group complain "We can't ever do that," they may actually be looking for reinforcement of their own capabilities.

It is for this reason that a planned performance may be incorporated into the activity. "We sounded so good on that, we really should sing it for someone else," may not be unanimously received, but if a situation is arranged with a minimum of stress (chairs in the front row of an audience, or a semicircle facing the rest of a large group instead of on a stage), the feeling of pride acknowledged afterward is well worth the trouble.

The Club

There are many residents in nursing home facilities who are very active and intellectually aware. They have previously enjoyed music; some may play instruments, and many love, or "used to love" to sing. For such people, a weekly music club or music appreciation group is a welcome addition to the activity schedule—a supplement to, rather than a replacement for, a sing-along.

The club may begin with an examination of music related to current events or folk music for holiday celebrations. A group may wish to study the origins of its members through ethnic music.

People who have been soloists in the past will probably be glad to share the words and melody of a song remembered. In one such club, after the group had heard the story of Carmen and listened to recorded excerpts, a former opera singer—now almost deaf—stood with a cane and treated the group to a rousing performance of the *Toreador Song*.

In the same group, a woman who obviously used to spend a lot of time playing piano for sing-alongs, would sandwich *Mary* in between every song the group decided to do. Since none of the residents seemed to mind this repetition, the pattern was continued. "We sang that already, but it's a grand old song, and she certainly likes to play it!"

Developing Group Support

In informal music groups, if a resident seems to have withdrawn and is chanting away, alone, the playing of the rhythm of that chant by members of the group, with instruments, will let the resident know that people are still with him or her, and still care enough to communicate.

One little lady, who was not oriented most of the time, always joined in the singing of *her* song, *Let Me Call You Sweetheart.* The whole group came together when this song was sung, because everyone was cooperating in the effort to "bring her back."

Another woman constantly complained "I don't know where I am," and the group usually responded with the old favorite, *Show Me the Way to Go Home.* Often such casual good humor offered by fellow group members is the best way to let someone know that he or she is not alone with a problem, and that others understand.

If a resident does not speak, or is unintelligible, a glance at the wrist identification tag may suggest an ethnic background. One woman, whose last name sounded German, not only joined all the words of *Du bist mein Hertzen,* but led the rest of the group in the singing.

One very old man came late to a large informal group on the ward and announced that he didn't like the songs the group was singing, but that *he* could play *I Love Coffee, I Love Tea* on the piano. Immediately, one of the women started singing all the lyrics to the tune, and all joined in once they heard the song. He was surprised to find out there were words to the music and happily accompanied the singers.

If a group member feels silly at being asked to play an instrument, another way to involve this person should be found. He or she may rather just sing, or in some cases take responsibility for the musical direction of the group. People who do not easily join an activity sometimes surprise themselves and the others by having a natural feeling for a downbeat. A baton lends even more significance to the position of conductor to start the group off and keep it together.

Staff Participation

Music groups, of course, are run for the benefit of the residents, not the staff on duty. But the positive attitude of the latter will help to create a sharing, often festive atmosphere, if they actually participate. This positive attitude may not always be evident when the activity is begun. The staff is busy, and after all the care they administer to the residents, they may find interruptions a burden, particularly if the activity occurs during their break. But if their participation is welcomed, they may prove a pleasant addition to the group.

In one nursing home, a cook joined the instrumental section with two of his best pan lids from the kitchen. In another, a nurse offered to teach the group a Spanish song. Aides who are free enjoy playing the more difficult melody instruments. And the patients, seen as equals in a situation like this, sing along with the them. They are sharing a social activity. It is no longer "We're the well ones and they're the sick ones."

Just as important is the attitude of alert residents toward group members who are disoriented. Often these alert residents tend to be somewhat exclusive, possibly because of the fear that "the same thing could happen to me." It is as if they will *catch* the lack of awareness, the regression, of another. They want the group leader to realize that they are not "like that" and do not wish to be associated with it. And this is possibly the same reason some members of the staff treat residents with more objectivity and less humanity than seems appropriate.

Reaching the Disoriented

Music is one realm in which people can be creative at any level of intellectual awareness. One group did Scottish songs for the members of the nursing home who were never brought to the weekly meetings because they were considered too disoriented. Curled up in a corner was a woman yelling nothing relevant in a high voice. She was given two small maracas which she played vigorously in time to the music. She enjoyed them so much that everyone in the room benefited from her pleasure.

It is amazing how such "disruptive" people can be "called back" with a simple, practical remark. When asked by name to join the singing instead of making noise that is interfering, they will often answer "All right," and begin to participate. If given an instrument, they will put all their energy into playing it. It makes one wonder if boredom is not at the root of much antisocial behavior. Or perhaps what we sometimes see is resistance against the passivity that is often encouraged in residential facilities.

It should never be assumed that someone does not want to participate. Rather, the search for a way to include that person should constantly be considered by the leader during the session and in between meetings.

Handling Individual Problems

If members of the group have assumed an active role in the structure of the activity, and if one patient does not wish to come to the meeting in the first place, but was wheeled or walked there by a member of the staff, his or her wish to leave is always respected. Or, if the prevalent attitude is "This is a special music group and that person is spoiling it," the person in question might be encouraged to leave a little early. However, a follow-up of the individual's interests is made, and an invitation to return and participate remains open.

Designing Personal Folders

Members may be given, or may help to prepare, folders of booklets containing the songs sung at group meetings. In the case of ethnic music workshops, songs and information about the different countries could be included. It is wise to have spare copies on hand for those who forget to bring them back. But just having them gives the group members a feeling of importance.

One resident I know keeps his music folder and a small flute used for sound effects, in the pouch attached to his walker. Others keep theirs to show visitors, and rarely bring them to meetings. Many have decorated their folders, and one woman designed a stencil to decorate all the folders in her group.

In some cases, a resident may know a song no one else knows. He or she adds to the resources of the group by giving the words to a member of the staff or by writing them down to be copied. A good idea suggested by members of many groups is to have all pages of such notebooks organized in the same manner, with the pages numbered.

Senior Centers

A substantial number of senior citizen centers have formed music groups. The most active members generally request the activity because of the many seniors who like to sing, and who play instruments.

Often, however, there are not quite enough people to achieve a good group sound, and there are few who will want to come on a regular basis. But if the nucleus is encouraged and asked to suggest songs for the group and to help develop general rehearsal procedure, those few will recruit others.

Respect Individuality

Working with older adults in music is in many ways similar to conducting a class for younger people. The same discrepancies in background and aptitude are encountered, the same difficulty of working with individuals in a group setting. But here, situations and people who seem very similar at first are often not at all similar. Two men who play the same instrument and come originally from the same foreign country may now live in different suburbs of the same city, have different life styles, and feel there is a world of difference between them. The leader should be aware of this and treat them as individuals.

But if a group of people of Italian descent can learn the words and music to a Portuguese song, it gives them a feeling of accomplishment, and it also gives the few Portuguese members in the group a special feeling of belonging.

The Leader

Perhaps the leader has presented a song from a particular book and a majority of the members say that the words of the song are "wrong." It is usually wise to alter the lyrics or have the members use pencils to make the changes themselves. In other musical matters, however, the leader must occasionally say "Do it this way." Indeed, if the group becomes too democratic, members who often remain quiet at meetings may come to the leader separately and request that the leader not let So-and-so run the group.

Some people feel embarrassed about singing alone, and some have never been part of an organized music group. They will come if they feel welcome, and if they feel their voices are blending in. If they express concern that their voices are too low, or that they cannot see the words easily, it is important to respond in a relaxed manner. Some casual remarks about the pleasant blending of high and low voices may be helpful. Be very supportive if you feel that a person actually knows most of the words already and does not need to read them, or suggest a little "lip-reading" if glasses are forgotten.

Range of Songs

Simple techniques such as *warming up* may be unknown to untrained vocalists, and many have negative ideas about vocalizing; but it is easy enough to choose a song in a comfortable range with few high notes until voices are sufficiently loose.

Some group members — and, in more cases, staff members — may complain that a song is too high or low.

If the leader is a trained musician, transposition should be easy enough, even though the written accompaniment has to be reduced to simple chords with the new symbols penciled in. However, if the leader is not the accompanist, and the accompanist is not proficient at transposition, the uncomfortable singers should be encouraged to put the melody down an octave, or to sing a harmony part. Nonprofessional leaders may be surprised to hear spontaneous harmonizing from members who find a pleasing way to blend their voices in a comfortable range. There is no need to make the accompanist, who may be a peer of the rest of the group, feel he or she is not making an important contribution to the group's activity.

The Space

In senior citizen centers, a piano in the space where the midday meal is served is a help, for informal music will always be welcome after lunch. Serious rehearsals in that space are very difficult to conduct before the meal. With all the noise of preparation and people coming in to eat, the music group is a source of aural competition.

Therefore, it is wise to consider seriously moving at least the initial

SARAH HOPKINS

meetings of a group into a smaller area, where the members will not feel self-conscious, and where the music in preparation may be discussed quietly.

Organization

As in working with people in nursing homes, clear presentation of material is particularly important. Song sheets clearly printed and arranged in a uniform way are necessary. Here, although the possibility also exists in nursing homes, the appointment of a secretary from the group to help keep things in order will certainly be well received. Other officers can help heighten spirit, interest, and attendance. Time should be spent as soon as possible after the creation of the group to discuss conducting techniques for those who would like to try to lead the singing. By reminding the senior who occasionally forgets reading glasses to bring them the next time, you remind that person to be responsible for personal needs.

SARAH HOPKINS

Performance

As soon as a group has prepared a few selections, a performance may be suggested. This can mean a few numbers after lunch, or a performance at a nearby nursing home. If relatives or friends of some of the members are in the home, a special sense of sharing is added.

A microphone will probably be necessary for the announcement of songs; and when possible, the members of the group should take turns making the introductions. They can choose which numbers they feel comfortable announcing, and should practice doing so at least once before the performance.

One senior group, at Thanksgiving time, performed in white pilgrim collars made from heavy white paper. At Christmas, red and green bows were added; and by St. Patrick's Day, the members decided to consider different costumes. Such discussions should not be allowed to take up the valuable rehearsal time of the group. But they should be considered afterward, because the members should be encouraged to make these decisions themselves.

In Conclusion

Since each group and each situation is different, it is probably unnecessary to offer more than a final word of encouragement to those of you who would like to take an active part in forming and/or participating in a music group with older people. Indeed, the most exciting thing that may happen to you may be your own musical growth and sense of enjoyment. As one staff member in a senior citizen center put it," Come and work with the seniors; they have a lot to teach you!"

SUGGESTED READINGS

Alvin, J. *Music therapy.* New York: Humanities Press, 1966.

Bright, J. *Music in geriatric care.* New York: St. Martin's Press, 1972.

Flutz, A. F. *Mot handbook.* Boston: Research Division of Musical Guidance, 1954.

Gaston, E. T., (Ed.), *Music in therapy.* New York: MacMillan Company, 1968.

The Journal of Music Therapy. National Association for Music Therapy, Inc.

Lippitt, R., Waton, J., & Westley, B. *The dynamics of planned change.* Harcourt, Brace & Company, Inc., 1958.

Priestley, M. *Music therapy in action.* New York: St. Martin's Press, 1975.

The challenge for the music therapist, as well as for all other staff members, is to restore to them healthy self-concepts . . . to convince them that there is a reason to live, that they still can make a contribution and enjoy life.

Marian D. Palmer, Registered Music Therapist; has a B.S. in Music Therapy and a B.A. in Applied Music. She has been the Coordinator of Therapy, Director of Music Therapy and Clinical Training Supervisor at Cedar Lake Home for the Aging, West Bend, Wisconsin. Speaker/consultant throughout the midwestern states, she is also a frequent contributor to major professional journals. She is Chairperson for the National Committee of Gerontology, National Association for Music Therapy; President of the Ohio Association for Music Therapy; on the Editorial Board of *Activities, Adaptation and Aging;* a producer of videotapes on the aging.

OLDER ADULTS ARE TOTAL PEOPLE
MUSIC THERAPY WITH THE ELDERLY

Marian Palmer, RMT

Music, the greatest good that mortals know, and
all of heaven that we have below.

Joseph Addison

If the quality of life for older adults is to be improved, if they are going to be helped to function at their maximum potential, they must be involved in a therapeutic program which meets their *total needs.* The music therapist who works in the field of gerontology today is concerned with the total person, and therefore develops programs which meet physical, mental, and psychosocial needs.

Unfortunately, most of the care provided for the elderly in extended care facilities is purely custodial, meeting their physical needs only, and most of the programs developed for the older adults in community-based settings is purely social, meeting those needs only. We in music therapy realize that people's needs are completely inter-related, and that if the mental and psychosocial ones are not met, the result will be physical deterioration. Here I will be discussing human needs in these three categories: physical, mental, and psychosocial, remembering that all three are being met in some degree in each music therapy session.

The Physical Condition

For most elderly adults, whether in a health care facility or in a community living situation, there is some physical impairment or debilitation which limits their activities of daily living to some degree. The basic goal of the music therapist, in this situation, is to evaluate the physical condition of the client and develop a treatment plan that will enable that person to become or remain as independent as possible. In some instances, the first goal is simply to counteract the contracture which develops when the resident sits with fists clenched and arms folded — a common posture of residents in nursing homes. Utilizing familiar music, the music therapist encourages the residents to relax while moving their arms back and forth in an "arm dancing" exercise.

One resident I worked with was of German descent. She was brought into the facility because she could no longer be cared for at home; she was too difficult to transfer and had no self-care skills. In the beginning she was in the posture described, head down and nonverbal. She struck out at anyone who disturbed her, which was her only use of the upper extremities. To counteract the contracture already apparent, I would play German folk-song records. When I put on a familiar German song she would visibly relax and allow me to straighten out her arms and move them back and forth in time to the music. Her arthritic fingers had to be straightened out and held in an open position to enable her to clap to a German polka, but she would allow this because she was so pleased to participate in this German music activity. Soon her head position improved as she would look up and smile at me and others in the group. In a few months she was even singing along in German!

As a result of this involvement she became able to assist in some daily living activities, such as raising her arms to brush her hair and wash her face. With an adaptive spoon she was again able to feed herself. However, perhaps, more important at least for the family, was the fact that she would smile and speak to them when they came for a visit. She was obviously enjoying life once more.

For many post-stroke clients rehabilitation is a matter of strengthening damaged muscles or restoring muscle tone through exercises. However, such physical exercise can be tiring and painful unless it is presented as part of an enjoyable music activity. For instance, playing maracas along with a mariachi band (on record) gives the resident an opportunity for movement of the upper extremities while joining peers on an imaginary trip to Mexico. For strengthening the oral muscles of a post-stroke victim, the melodica provides an enjoyable and rewarding experience, while improving the muscles needed for regaining speech.

Involvement in an eurhythmic session, (rhythmic movement to music) using either hoops or batons can also provide muscle-toning exercise while creating entrancing patterns to music. This is particularly reinforcing when done in front of a mirror where the members of the group can have the immediate satisfaction of seeing the patterns they can create. In larger groups, the upper extremities can be effectively exercised by utilizing a maypole.

This maypole is placed in the center of the group, which may be composed of both ambulatory and nonambulatory residents, and a ribbon given to each member of the group. Again the movements to the music are demonstrated by the music therapist who improvises whatever movements are needed for the proper exercise in this situation. This also affords an opportunity to reinforce color concepts, if appropriate for the group. The maypole can be made by the residents themselves, using ribbon from floral bouquets. This offers both a purposeful activity and an opportunity for peer interaction. In this situation total needs are met, although the primary goal is physical activity.

Fine motor coordination is often improved by utilizing musical instruments such as the autoharp, guitar, or keyboard. The music therapist works at the functioning level of the client, developing color or number-coded scores for those unable to read the traditional musical score. With the development of Orff instruments which require only minimal ability, a musical device, such as striking a tone bell, anyone can be included. The joy of making music with others becomes the motivation to improve the physical functioning of those involved.

The Mental Condition

In the area of mental functioning, the goal for those in most extended-care facilities is to maintain contact with reality. The work done in reality orientation classes has been proven to be quite ineffective unless reinforced on a 24-hour basis. This involves the support of the entire staff; and the music therapist therefore uses reality orientation techniques in all sessions. However, some music therapy sessions are specifically geared to this concept when it is seen to be the primary need of the individuals involved. The session may be, on the surface, a simple sing-a-long; however, under the direction of the music therapist it becomes an occasion for recalling songs of the past, putting them in the proper time perspective, and helping the residents make and maintain contact with the present. Learning new songs is also an opportunity for them to redevelop memory skills which may not have been used for years.

The music therapist can also reinforce color concepts, body concepts, and spatial concepts where appropriate, and can help orient the residents to the season of the year with appropriate seasonal music. With a higher functioning group the session can provide good mental exercise as they recall songs beginning with the letters of the alphabet or songs connected with famous people. In any of these sessions the goal is to stimulate mental functioning, recognizing that the brain, also, falls into the category of "use it or lose it." Higher functioning residents can also be involved in song-writing sessions, which provide them with the opportunity not only for good mental exercise but also for a new and successful experience, especially when the song they have written is performed by the choir or some other performing group. Again, these sessions are providing enjoyable social experiences while concentrating mainly on the goal of improved mental functioning.

Frequently, the confused arteriosclerotic resident in a nursing home does not know the names of others in the same area. Sometimes they have difficulty remembering their own names. With these residents the music therapist often utilizes a song at the beginning of the session which calls each of them by name. They enjoy being singled out for this attention and are pleased with the individual recognition.

With this type of resident I frequently end the session by asking how many are in the group, giving them a chance to practice their counting skills, and also encouraging once again their looking at one another. They then join hands for the final number, which provides warm interaction and develops a community spirit. As they become more aware of one another and as they develop a sense of belonging to a group, they become more accepting of their new life-style. This change in attitude often results in a great improvement in their physical well-being as well as their mental and social functioning.

The Psychosocial Condition

The psychosocial needs of the older adult presents what I believe to be the greatest challenge. For the most part, our society has, in a variety of ways, made it clear to them that they are inferior beings or in some instances, nonpersons. Many of them have lost not only their significant role in society and significant others in their lives, but also some physical and mental functioning ability. All of this results in a damaged ego. The challenge for the music therapist, as well as for all other staff members, is to restore to them healthy self-concepts. If they have suffered severe losses they are frequently no longer interested in living and will withdraw into a world of their own, hoping to die. The challenge in this situation is to convince them that there is a reason to live, that they still can make a contribution and can also find enjoyment in life, no matter what their functioning level.

Since music has been part of the experience of everyone, it becomes an excellent means of drawing these residents back into the present world. The music therapist often has to delve into the background of the resident, to find out what has been enjoyed in the past, what interests and what talents were shown, so that a program can be developed which will speak to the needs of that particular resident.

There was one woman who lay in a fetal position, seemingly nonverbal and totally unresponsive. Her family mentioned that she had always loved baseball, and would listen to the games. One of the housekeeping staff noticed that during the music therapy sessions she would open her eyes and watch me when I was not looking her way. Individual attention and the song *Take Me Out to the Ball Game* eventually brought a response. By working with her gently and patiently we were able to bring her into the group, not only to sing along and to enter into the conversation but also to use her good right arm to play a rhythm instrument. During these sessions her body would straighten out and she would endeavor to participate in all the movements to the extent of her ability. This improvement in functioning tranferred to her other activities of daily living. As she became more alert and more involved, her physical condition improved. She simply needed a reason to come out of her shell and be part of a world she had totally rejected.

In another situation I worked with a group of residents where the goal was to help them overcome negative attitudes. In each instance there was much physical deterioration, although the mental functioning level was high. The trauma of going from totally independent persons who had lived fruitful and active lives, to dependence on others even for their most personal needs had been too much for them to accept. The result was a group of negative, hostile, and mostly nonverbal residents, who were totally unaccepting of the change in their lives.

I tried to get them to interact with each other, to share their feelings and their experiences. By using familiar music of their day I tried to evoke some memories and get them talking with one another. Eventually they found that they had much in common and they began transcribing their feelings into songs. This turned into a particularly gratifying experience when they wrote a song about their state which was sent to the governor who wrote them a letter of commendation for the fine state song. This then led to involvement in other activities and other satisfying experiences. They learned that, in spite of physical limitations, they still had much to contribute to life, and to gain in return.

One man came to our facility with a diagnosis of terminal cancer. He was admitted to our intensive care unit, totally unable to care for himself. With the support of the entire staff we were able to explain to him that although his diagnosis was terminal cancer, it might take a long time. In the meantime it was a beautiful day outside and there was much going on he could enjoy if he would come out of his bed and his room. He was a music buff, and after listening to a few rehearsals of the band, he joined, and became the leader of the maracas section. At Christmastime he was one of the Wise Men in the pageant put on by the residents.

Three years later he is thoroughly enjoying life and now resides in the residential area where he is mostly self-care and quite independent. This highly intelligent, delightful man has learned that dying can take a long time, so living each day to the utmost makes a lot of sense. The physical diagnosis has not changed but his attitude has. He is no longer waiting to die — he is enjoying living.

Many residents have lost their significant role in the larger community, but they can be helpful to assume an important role in this new one. They can join a performing group, such as a choir, band, or drum corps; they can develop their talents to play instruments for performance. Sometimes the residents need encouragment to relearn old skills, such as playing the piano or singing. In any case, the goal is to provide them with new opportunities for success.

Frequently, the residents can assume leadership roles in their new community by leading groups or functioning as librarian for the choir. As they assume these responsible roles in their new living situation they accept a different life-style and develop a more affirmative attitude towards life itself. This improves not only their psychosocial behavior but also their mental and physical functioning. They are able to attain and then maintain their highest level of functioning for a long time, and once again enjoy a worthwhile quality of life.

In the Community

For the elderly who remain in the community, the music therapist working through community centers offers the same opportunity to find new roles and new ways to contribute. Programs are developed to provide purposeful activity for those who are mentally alert and physically capable. Without such stimulus they may slip into early deterioration because they are not in an environment which encourages them to be the *most* of themselves. Here again the therapist draws on the experiences of their past in order to design a program which will meet their present and future needs. Some of these elderly find enjoyment in joining such things as an "alumni" barbershop group or a bell choir. For some, performance is not appealing but they enjoy a music appreciation group which attends performances in the community and then discusses the music and the instruments involved. Again, since music has been part of their past experience it becomes a very natural way to help them find new and enjoyable activities for these latter years.

One final note: It has always been my practice to end every music therapy session, regardless of the functioning level of the resident, with an individual handshake or hug for each member in the group along with a sincere "thank you" for their contribution, whatever it might have been. This individual attention and recognition by name is, I believe, of paramount importance since they have so few opportunities in their lives to be recognized and thanked for a job well done. More and more we are beginning to recognize the therapeutic value of physical touch in working with the elderly and this meets that need.

Older adults are total people with total needs which must be met if they are to function at maximum potential. The music therapist recognizes this and plans a treatment program which will meet those requirements. It may be through a group session where the needs of the members of the group are similar, or it may be through individual sessions. In every case they are the basis for the program which is implemented. Progress towards the stated goals is carefully documented so that new goals may be established when appropriate. Only in this way can the therapist be sure that the needs are indeed being met, and that the desired improvement is taking place. When this procedure is followed the result is an improved quality of life for each one involved in a music therapy session . . . and that is the basic goal of every music therapist.

Coda

One of the interesting sidelights to music therapy programs with the elderly is the reaction of the families involved. Frequently the involvement of the resident becomes the bridge towards better communication with the family. A typical instance occurred recently with a group of residents in a local nursing home. Our music therapy sessions were culminating in a spring musicale in which several of the residents would be doing solo work. The invitation was sent out to all the families inviting them to attend. One of the soloists had not had a visit from his family in 10 years but they came to the event and were thrilled to see him in this role. During the social hour afterwards, they visited and showed pictures of the grandchildren and promised to come often. The old uncomfortable visits were forgotten in light of this new relationship.

SUGGESTED READINGS

Caplow-Lindner, E., Harpaz, L., & Samberg, S. *Therapeutic dance-movement — Expressive activities for older adults.* New York: Human Sciences Press, 1979.

DePeters, J., Gordan, L., & Wertman, A. *The magic of music.* Buffalo, New York: Potentials Development.

Heidenreich, Sister L. *Advanced eurhythmics.* Elm Grove, Wisconsin: Notre Dame Health Care Center. (This is a workbook of procedures developed and used with the elderly in the Notre Dame Health Care Center).

Heidenreich, Sister L. *Eurhythmic gestures.* Elm Grove, Wisconsin: Notre Dame Health Care Center. (This is a workbook of procedures developed and used with the elderly in the Notre Dame Health Care Center).

Merrill, T. *Discussion topics for oldsters in nursing homes.* Springfield, Illinois: Charles C. Thomas Publishing Co., 1974.

Working with the elderly, group processes and techniques. Belmont, California: Duxbury Press, Wadsworth Publishing Company, 1978.

PART III

DANCE AND MOVEMENT: A PRIMARY ART EXPRESSION

Dance and movement represent the earliest and most basic expression of human emotion. They reveal the universal symbols and rituals of our primitive selves. Our authors in this section discuss the effectiveness of their art form with seniors as it evokes active participation in community and institutional settings.

Jocelyn Helm is a dance therapist and educator whose experiences as the director of a senior resource center give her a special perspective on the total needs of the elderly. She traces the development of a program she conceptualized for the community and she shares innumerable ideas for working on specific physical problems with individuals in her movement workshops.

Dorothy Jungels and John Belcher work together as a dance and music team who also call on art and poetry in their relationships with elderly in a mental institution. Lively anecdotes illustrate how their contrapuntal use of the arts can affect change even when it is most unexpected.

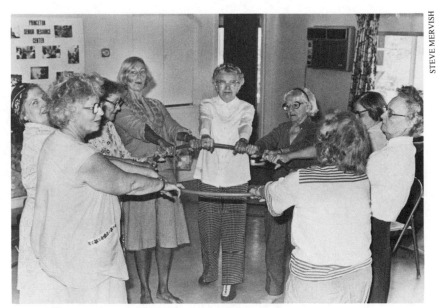

A Dance Therapy session at the Senior Resource Center, Princeton, N.J.

When we know our feelings, we know who we are.
When we accept our feelings, we accept ourselves.
When we think of ourselves as 'our bodies,' we can
move through life with grace and dignity.

Jocelyn Helm, M.A. Educational Dance, DT; is Director of the Princeton Resource Center, Princeton, New Jersey. She leads regular workshops with senior adults in therapeutic movement. She also trains professionals and paraprofessionals in psychosocial approaches to their populations through movement. Mrs. Helm is President of the Gerontological Society of New Jersey, 1983; New Jersey delegate to the National Institute of Senior Centers, National Council on Aging; a member of the NCOA Convention Committee, Detroit, 1983. She is on the Advisory Board, National Educational Council of Creative Therapies. She was elected to the Governor's Advisory Council for the 1981 White House Conference on Aging.

Chapter 7

"CAN YOU GRAB A STAR?"
DANCE/MOVEMENT IN A SENIOR RESOURCE CENTER

by Jocelyn Helm

Our dance/movement group at the Senior Resource Center has been described as "just a little bit crazy" by those who peek in the door or happen to overhear little bits of conversation:

Float your arms sl-o-o-w-ly up to the sky.
Can you stretch up and grab a star?
Now pull — pull that star down — harder, now!

or

Let's make some funny faces!
Answer: *You don't need to — You already have one!*

or

Give yourself a big hug.
Answer: *I'd rather hug you than hug myself.*

or

You own all the space you can reach — Pull it all in around you and shape it into anything you would like — Can we explore some of that space behind us?

Answer provided by a ninety year-old group member:

I'll be exploring that space soon enough without this!

The students, who range to ninety-nine years of age, are urged to bend, stretch, clap, flick, punch, shake, pull, and toss imaginary but also some real objects. They begin to loosen up and respond to their bodies. Feelings and memories are freed; repressed anger and sorrow begin to emerge and they become involved in the life around them. Contact is being made with both their emotions and their physical bodies as the group progresses through movements designed to reawaken the "child" in them and shake out the rust of body disuse. One has only to survey the scene and note the intensity of the self-expression and communication taking place to see the well-nigh universal myths and stereotypes about our elderly dissolving.

Why is it that those things which we think of as antique are cherished and revered, while the word "old" renders an entirely different connotation? If you ask a group of people to respond to the word "old," what you hear is "discarded," "used," "fragile," and "worn out." These meanings are commonly applied to today's rapidly growing population of elderly and thus we can understand why there is so little motivation on their part to change their second-rate status in society. Many seniors have been receiving the message for the past 50 years, and they believe it.

Some years ago my work began as an intern in Dance Therapy at a New York Hospital focused on the elderly. Most of the members in my sessions were over sixty. Many of these people didn't seem too different from what I term the "normal neurotic," but they were not young, and they had fallen into a semidependent state and there was nowhere for them to go.

My interest was aroused, and I decided that I would devote my energies and insights as a dance therapist to develop a better understanding of movement as a resource for the elderly. This is an area which holds great fascination for me, since I was, and am, faced daily with the reality that many older people refuse to accept the responsibility for their own physical and mental well-being. Many of them who do have aches and pains use these discomforts as an excuse to sit back and do nothing. Society then reinforces the "don't overdo" attitude and gradually the message reads "sit down and take it easy."

Why not attempt a different program of physical activity which would combine within a community setting my training in physical education, movement rehabilitation and dance therapy? Most exercise programs which have been developed for the elderly have focused on the cardiovascular and respiratory systems. Research does support the observation that exercise increases cardiac and vascular fitness, and, significantly, that this improvement does not depend on having trained vigorously in youth. It has been substantiated that exercise, especially proper breathing exercises, can strengthen the respiratory muscles, provide better ventilation, and increase the vital capacity of the lungs.

During the past few years a new approach, "Gerokinesiatrics," defined as the use of movement or exercise in the treatment of diseases of aging, has been emerging. Some physicians have become interested and involved in helping people function within the confines of many debilitating illnesses. Diseases which accompany old age such as emphysema, Parkinson's disease, arthritis, other joint diseases, and depression, have become the target. Doctors are beginning to view the older person as a *whole* person who is *alive* rather than someone who is dying from a disease called *old age*!

In a paper presented at a meeting of The Gerontological Society of New Jersey, Dr. Stanley J. Brody, Department of Physical Medicine and Rehabilitation, University of Pennsylvania, claimed that perhaps one-third of the sixty-five-plus population suffers from depression at one time or another with perhaps 5 to 6 per cent suffering from senile dementia. This is not such an astounding figure when you become aware of the fact that as you age you have fewer reserves with which to ward off the multiplicity of physical and psychological insults.

Depression, then, is a natural consequence. The beneficial effects of exercise and movement are now beginning to be understood. For example, there is evidence that half an hour of exercise can have the same calming effect as a typical dose of a tranquilizer. With growing widespread drug abuse among the elderly, why not try some different approaches?

Movement as a Holistic Tool

The question most often asked of me is, "What is so different about your program of dance/movement?" My answer is that movement is used as a tool to involve the whole person so that older people can use their bodies as instruments for release and joy. Where is the child in us which we have repressed for so many years? What seems to be missing in many of the national programs is a sense of fun and companionship.

I am convinced that you cannot persuade a person of considerable years to take part in a program simply because it is "good for you." As children we never bought that rationale and certainly very few older adults will respond to this approach.

Dr. James Sheehan, a cardiologist who has become the "guru" of runners on the East Coast, speaks also of the "child" in us and the benefits of allowing that part (the creative part) to be released through movement. The dance/movement group can provide a safe, supportive, nonthreatening atmosphere where people can be alive and experience validation through sharing personal insights.

There is little to prepare us for the experience of growing old. When we discuss this in the group, most of the clients speak of how they feel the same as they did when they were in their twenties except that their bodies do not function as well. We try to expand their body-movement range in order to restore self-awareness.

Older people are beginning to realize that aging and chronic disease are not synonymous. Dance is one of the tools that sustains life—a tool by which withdrawal, loneliness, and the depression of old age can be dispelled. When we know our feelings, we know who we are; when we accept our feelings, we accept ourselves. When we think of ourselves as "our body," we can move through life with grace and dignity.

The following are some thoughts on dance/movement by a seventy-eight year-old woman who has participated in our program for over 5 years:

> When I do the dance/movements which are quite varied, I experience feelings of release and pleasure. I know while doing them that they are good for the functioning of my body and keep it moving more easily, and I also receive good feelings that I am keeping my mind active in a certain way! Plus the knowledge that I am part of a community effort.

She had very limited and bound patterns of movement when she first joined the group. She has gradually expanded her "movement vocabulary" through the use of tasks, themes, and imagery, to the point where her whole spectrum of movement has been widened, and she is beginning to rediscover her full potential.

Setting up Dance/Movement Programs

In order to set up a community dance/movement program, there are many questions to be considered. The five most important challenges which I faced were:

Funding: local, state, and federal sources.

Location: a central location which can be reached easily by public transportation, if any. (During the first 2 years of my program there was no public transportation in our town.)

Publicity: publicizing the program and attracting members.

Group Composition: selecting the specific population.

Community Support: involving other agencies in the community so that they work with the program rather than compete with it.

Funding and Location

Funding was the most immediate concern, and after investigating many private and state institutions, I found that they were not interested in programs such as this unless they were time-fillers and I would work as a volunteer. I received advice such as "perhaps if you give us your time for awhile, you can work into a part-time position."

My focus then moved toward funding possibilities from the state and federal government. A request for a proposal was being circulated by the State Division on Aging, Department of Community Affairs, to involve Public Housing Authorities which had empty community rooms (no funds having been provided to staff them) to stimulate programs for their elderly residents. What an opportunity to solve both the problem of funding and location! Imagine having a captive audience with whom to form the core.

Our proposal was approved. It was one of the 12 Housing Authorities (Department of Housing and Urban Development) in 1972 to be funded by the New Jersey State Department of Community Affairs for a demonstration program.

Publicity

With the problems of funding and location out of the way, I could then focus on publicizing and trying to attract members to the group. Program information can be disseminated in many ways but the most effective way is to interest a few people and have them act as your publicity agents—word of mouth is by far the easiest and most efficient method.

However, you can not rely on this alone. All media you can use are helpful. Newspapers and radio usually have weekly senior calendars and are willing to include any information. Demonstrations can be given in the community—especially to groups which cater to senior citizen's activities (AARP, YWCA, Senior Citizens' Clubs, Business and Professional Women's Clubs, Jewish Center and various church organizations). After a successful demonstration, there are always enthusiastic promises, but with the dawning of a new day plagued by bad weather, poor transportation, and chronic disorders, the good intentions often dissolve.

Group Composition

For many years the medical profession tended to lump all the elderly into one category. It has been a difficult lesson which programmers in the aging network have had to unlearn. More and more literature is now being written on the wide individuality of the elderly population which received few, if any, services. I tried to attract the older, less active group. The important factor to emphasize is the adaptability of dance/movement which allows individuals to participate at their own levels.

Our group is composed of approximately 20 members with anywhere from 6 to 15 showing up for each session. Of these 20 members, six remain from the original core group, and three have died. Three clients have serious emphysema, five are afflicted with arthritis or stiffness in the joints, one is recovering from an auto accident, two have slight cardiovascular problems, and the rest attend for the sociability.

"I come here to satisfy my skin hunger!" one of the group members exclaimed. What a wonderfully insightful, feeling statement. Ashley Montague, the anthropologist, speaks of our culture as a nation of untouchables, unable to express affection or understand the language of touch. Maggie Kuhn, Founder of the Gray Panthers, calls herself "the wrinkled radical" and berates people by saying, "Touch me—wrinkles aren't contagious."

One member, ninety-nine years old, found that she could not come during the winter months, and is now too debilitated by osteoporosis. I visit her often and she confesses to tapping her feet and moving her fingers and hands so that she will not just "moulder away like some people around here!" Another member, who was a visitor for 2 years from Great Britain, had suffered a stroke. She was greatly excited by our program and felt it was instrumental in helping her regain some of her functioning. She was intent on getting back to her home town to spread the word of what wonders had occurred. One member says that she has substantially reduced her "widow's hump" through a series of back exercises. A third member, eighty-four, describes her feelings: "I love to close my eyes, listen to the music and get the rhythm going in my body—like the trees swaying outside. One gets that floating feeling with no worry or care. The music is good today. I'd like to get up and dance the way I used to at the Rochester Exposition."

Scheduling

Our group meets twice a week in midmorning. Although the elderly have more time for leisure and the pursuit of expressive roles, they tend to spend little time actively engaged in creative and intellectual pursuits. One of the first things I learned was to schedule around the soap operas, for out of an average of 5 leisure daytime hours, many seniors spend at least one-half this time watching TV. Regular meeting times are established and group members are encouraged to make a real commitment of time to the program so that the sessions become an integral part of their lives. I find that even those members with problems of memory and confusion manage to attend on a regular basis.

Community Support

In order to involve other agencies in the community and convince them of the benefits of a dance/movement program, I had to do a great deal of consciousness-raising and advocacy. My presentations concentrated on the importance of physical activity throughout the entire life span, not as a stopgap measure when you reach sixty years. Somehow the value of physical exercise is lost as we enter the middle years; we become spectators.

Educating the public to the value of any kind of commitment to a lifelong program of movement and exercise is a very difficult task. The focus of the health service industry has never been on prevention. We must promote programs of exercise as a process by which we can maintain a healthy, alert, and independently active life. Too many older people follow their physician's advice to the letter. When a doctor says "take it easy," he or she doesn't mean to vegetate and become stagnant. The term "hypokinetic disease" has been coined by Kraus and Raab and is defined as the whole spectrum of somatic and mental derangements caused by inactivity.[1]

Considerations for Early Sessions

The dance therapist must be constantly alert to the fears, frustrations, and limitations of his or her population. When moving hurts, one moves less. There is loss in motility and a resultant loss in muscle tone. Obesity and fat encasing the muscles make movement even more difficult. Fears of falling, heart attack, and pain are all realities. Many elderly who are physically inactive often have a very distorted body image. They think of themselves as being broader and heavier, and often feel the activity to be more strenuous than it is in reality. This can lead to a clumsiness which in turn completes the cycle by increasing fears.

Dr. Robert Havighurst, Professor of Education and Human Development, University of Chicago, has stated that the three needs of the elderly are stimulation, identity, and security. I find that this is an excellent foundation for dance/movement sessions. The definition of dance therapy as "the psychotherapeutic use of movement as a process which furthers the emotional and physical integration of the individual," spells out the concerns of the movement therapist. Stimulation and identity are my prime target.

Yes, I use that lost language of *touch* as much as possible to show that the group cares. Although the tactile sense is the most important of the senses (skin being the largest organ of the body), the elderly rarely experience the warmth of a gentle hug or caress. I also encourage creativity in every possible way. How moving it is to see the smiles of pure enjoyment as we form imaginary shapes which conjure up memories of the past. These, in turn, are designed to stimulate and increase the blood flow, but also to activate the mental processes. A healthy mix of both verbal and nonverbal communications takes place spontaneously.

When dealing with individual identities, it is essential to provide a congruent and accepting atmosphere in which the group members can express both positive and negative feelings. Even though we use the group as support, each person's individuality is respected. Their *own* movements are important. No one is judged on performance or endurance. Virtuosity is not the aim.

Screening Individuals

The proper screening of all individuals is extremely important. The type of exercise appropriate for the elderly person varies greatly according to age, physical condition, and personal preferences. Factors that should be known about participants include:

1. Risk factor assessment—information received from a doctor; results from an electrocardiagram; ongoing medical assessment
2. Past athletic participation
3. Amount of present physical activity
4. Presence of heart disease in family
5. Weight problems
6. Existence of hypertension
7. Personal habits, e.g., smoking, drinking

The geriatric dance/movement sessions which I lead are based upon knowledge of the biological changes which take place during the aging process. There is a general slowing down in the human organism. The body gradually loses its ability to renew itself, and there are marked changes in the sensory processes. Some particulars of the aging process are as follows:

1. An increase of connective tissues. Linkages form between the connective tissues, which leads to a loss of their elastic properties.
2. A disappearance of the cellular elements in the nervous system. The neuron fails to reproduce itself and thus there is a reduction in the number of normally functioning cells.
3. An increase in intercellular sludge which impairs cell functions.
4. An increase in fat accumulation—more fat stored in the muscles.
5. A decrease in hormonal output.
6. A decrease in muscle strength.
7. A decrease in cardiac output at rest, particularly in the cerebral blood flow.
8. There is a slowing of reaction time.
9. There is some memory loss—especially short term.
10. A decrease in breathing capacity of the lungs and thus a marked decrease in oxygen utilization.
11. Greater water retention at the expense of solid elements.
12. The autoimmune response mechanism appears to turn against itself and often treats other parts of the body as foreign invaders.
13. There is a shift in the center of gravity, particularly in women, which often causes problems with balance. Falls are the sixth largest cause of death in the elderly.
14. A decrease in calcium so that the bones become brittle and porous. Often the bones become compressed and deformed as with osteoporosis.
15. There is a different reaction to drugs and to combinations of drugs. Because drugs are stored in the fat cells and there is an increase in those cells, there is a different drug management problem.

In light of these many changes, I find myself consciously using certain group leadership techniques:

Speaking and articulating carefully and slowly.
Maintaining as much eye contact as possible.
Demonstrating clearly so that everyone can see.
Repeating a comment made by one group member so that each person hears it.
Making each member aware of the other members' disabilities so that each is sensitive to the others' needs.
Interspersing the session with plenty of relaxation and breathing exercises.
Using sequences of movements which stimulate use of the memory.
Using series of movements which require concentration and coordination.

A Typical Geriatric Dance Therapy Session

Participants
1. Men and women sixty-five years or older in wheelchairs or ambulatory.
2. Ideal number, eight to twelve.

Location
A large room. This gives an atmosphere of freedom. Space and good ventilation are essential. Often the elderly experience temperature changes acutely. If the space is too big, a room divider can be used.

Equipment
1. Phonograph and records. The music should be related to the participants. Often they prefer something with a strong rhythmic beat. Ethnic music, such as Greek, Polish, Israeli, etc.
2. Folding chairs with straight backs placed in a circle.
3. Mats for those who are willing to get down on the floor.
4. Piano—we are lucky to have a piano player. Whenever possible live music is preferable. Often, you can draw upon the senior population for a piano player.

Props
1. Scarves, hoops, ropes, balloons, feathers, masks, and mirrors can be used to explore space.
2. Rhythm instruments, such as maracas, bongos, tambourines, sticks. Often, when participants don't want to move, they are willing to involve themselves by keeping time with the instruments.
3. Three-foot smooth sticks often can be used to manipulate the limbs, and

are very helpful with stretching and twisting.
4. Balls, both large and small. The small balls are excellent for limbering the fingers, wrists, and hands. The largest balls are good for practicing coordination. I like the wool balls the best, and they are easily made by the seniors. They are so soft that no one can get hurt.
5. A parachute; or, if you can't afford one, sew two double sheets together.

Methods and Sequence

1. Explanation of our contract:
   They work to their own capacity and within their limitations.
   They can stop anytime.
   No one is judging, so they don't have to worry about how they look.
   They must make a commitment to the group.
2. Begin by socializing and getting acquainted. Memory games with names are fun and help to break the ice.
3. Warming up: experience the different body parts; where they are and how they feel.
   Listen to the music.
   Feel the beat or pulse.
   Start by *tapping* or *moving* different parts of the feet: toes, balls, heels.
   Travel up body by using each part alone: shoulders, elbows, arms, wrists, hands, fingers, eye exercises, making faces, neck rolls, etc.
   Slap different areas of the body while identifying them, starting at the bottom and working up from toes and feet to include head, face and neck massage to *wake up* the different parts.
4. Stretches: more exploration and experiencing; active and passive manipulation.
   Pushing head up to ceiling—centering.
   Articulating vertebrae by *uncurling* and *curling*.
   Stretching arms up to ceiling, one side, then the other.
   Twisting through the torso.
   Opening and *closing* rib cage stretches.
   Reaching out across the circle to one another and pulling. Group interaction, using props and visual imagery.
5. Breathing: one or two of these exercises when the participant needs to slow down and relax. Intersperse them throughout the session.
   Opening and *closing*—inhale as you open, exhale as you close.
   Uncurling—start in a curled position and slowly *uncurl*.
   Slowly *hiss* the air out of the body, then *float* with eyes closed by slowly pulling air in through the nose and mouth filling the stomach like a balloon. Then hiss it out twice as slowly through the mouth.
6. Discovering and experiencing feelings.
   Stimulate all parts of the body by mimicking the movements suggested by

each member of the group. Suggest movements at first which are familiar so they begin to reminisce, i.e., "How did you churn the butter?" Can we all try churning?"

Help them improvise a dance to which they can relate, i.e., Charleston, Alley Cat, Square Dances.

Encourage movements which incorporate some of these efforts,* i.e. strong, light, quick punching, flicking, dabbing, slashing, kicking, floating, are all movements which they can do with feeling.

7. Winding Down—pulling the session together.

Let the group experience mutual support.

Rock up and out of the chairs.

Swaying together.

Holding hands and *swinging*.

Balancing on toes—*holding* on to each other.

Reaching upwards as high as possible.

Knee bends (slight) and *balancing* on one foot.

Swinging legs gently and *moving* in close to form a small circle.

Touching, hugging, patting, kissing, are the way we say good-bye!

Everyone is urged to take these exercises and techniques home with them. They can do many of them while watching TV or lying in their beds.

Conclusions

Services provided for the elderly usually focus only on the most basic physical needs. Most of the therapeutic efforts are directed toward curing specific conditions, and not toward the overall needs of the individual. The aged lose their identity and become medical management problems. Often they adopt the "sick role" in order to live up to the expectations of society. This depersonalizing atmosphere offers no gratification, and serves only to reinforce the isolation and the separation that is often the cause for institutionalization.

It is important for dance therapists to be knowledgeable about these problems of the elderly if we are actively to advocate and promote the development and funding of new programs in our communities. We can add a major dimension to the field of dance therapy through the development of specific new programs of movement which will help integrate the individual both physically and psychologically. Senior centers, nutrition sites, rehabilitation centers, nursing homes and community-based psychiatric facilities can benefit from these programs which are geared to meet the individual needs of the elderly.

We, as creative arts therapists, are convinced that such programs, if effectively supported, can have a significant preventive effect in reducing the cost of health care by reducing the resident population in our mental institutions, as well as improving the quality of life for the elderly. "The tragedy of old age in America is that we have made absurdity all but inevitable. We have cheated ourselves. But we still have the possibility of making life a work of art."[2]

NOTES

[1]Woodruff, D.S., & Birren, J.E. *Aging, scientific perspectives and social issues*, New York: D. Van Nostrand Co., 1975.

[2]Butler, R.N.*Why survive? Being old in America*, New York: Harper and Row, 1975.

*Effort-Shape — A system of organic movement designed by Rudolph Laban

SUGGESTED READINGS

Curtain, S.R. *Nobody ever died of old age*. Boston, Massachusetts: G.K. Hall and Co., 1973.

de Beauvior, S. *The coming of age*. New York: G.P. Putnam's Sons, 1972.

DeVries, H. Physiological effects of an exercise training regimen upon men aged 52-88. *Journal of Gerontology*, 1970.

Helm, J.B., & Gill, K.L. An essential resource for the aging: Dance therapy. *Dance Research Journal. CORD*. vii:I. Fall-Winter 1974-75.

Laban, R. *The mastery of movement*,(3rd ed.). Boston: Plays, Inc., 1971.

President's Council on Aging *Fitness in the later years*. . Washington: Department of Health, Education and Welfare. 1968. Microfilm.

Preuss, K. *Life time, a new image of aging*. Santa Cruz, California: Unity Press, 1978.

Rosenberg, M. *Sixty-plus and fit again. Exercises for older men and women*. Boston, Massachusetts: G.K. Hall & Co., 1978.

*Art programs encourage these expressions, allow a
time for them to happen, media for them to happen
through, space for them to be arranged, rearranged,
expanded or modified, and present an ear, an
audience.*

Dorothy Jungels, B.A. Art; has been Director of the Rhode Island School of Design Dance
Concerts; and the Rhode Island State Council on the Arts Touring Show for nursing homes and
senior citizen sites where she also leads workshops. She has been a performer in the series called
Sunday Nights in the Park, the All Tap Revue, and the Rhode Island Ballet Theatre. She has
choreographed several documentary films including *Oh How We Danced!*, about social dance in
Rhode Island and Rhode Island dance halls. She is a dance teacher in the Rhode Island schools
and the Dorothy Jungels School of Ballet. As an artist, Ms. Jungels has illustrated *Nine on a
String*, a primary supplementary reader, published by Ginn & Co. Her sculpture exhibits have
appeared in Nantucket, New York City, Texas, and Washington, D.C.

John M. Belcher, B.S. Applied Math; is a musician, recording artist, and teacher. He works in
the Providence, Rhode Island area nursing homes and senior citizen centers; the Institute of Mental Health; Providence Public Schools and at the Rhode Island Junior College, Division of Continuing Education. Mr. Belcher teaches classes of mentally, physically, and emotionally disturbed
children. He also does consulting for colleges and hospitals. His film work includes the
documentary, *Oh How We Danced!* and *Art and the Aging: Dance*, a video documentary, with
Dorothy Jungels.

"MY CHEEKS ARE ROSY ANYWAY; I CAN'T BE DEAD"
A MULTI-ARTS PROGRAM AT A MENTAL INSTITUTION

by Dorothy Jungels
with John Belcher

> In nature a tiny particle is as beautiful and important as a star. Man was the first who presumed to judge what was beautiful and what was ugly.
>
> Hans Arp

The Arts and the Aging Program of the Rhode Island State Council on the Arts was continually searching for ways to bring artists and the arts to older people in the community. We artists were inspired, delighted, and touched by the opportunity to be with the older people. We found that no matter at what age, they responded to the arts and the opportunities to express themselves. John, a musician, and I were hired at first to lead music and dance classes; eventually we included art and writing. We were sent all over the state to nursing homes, lunch sites, senior citizen clubs and housing, and even to choreograph for a group of ladies in their seventies called "The Gingham Girls."

A Mental Hospital

Our program director, Margot Honig, found that the state mental hospital was filled with elderly people, and that there were not many art programs available to them. We were asked to lead sessions on the wards.

As we discovered, mental institutions are usually large, off by themselves somewhere, a place to be hidden, lost, and forgotten. Many old people have been there since youth. They have experienced and somehow survived shock treatments, lobotomies, and in some places, mistreatment, such as being dressed in nothing but hospital johnnies and left to defecate in floor drains.

We had had no previous exposure to the bleakness of a locked ward. When John and I entered the room filled with old women in cotton housedresses, it was frightening. Maybe a big factor was the missing teeth and straight hair that at first sight made them look like witches. One large lady who had scared us initially, in time became our close friend. She insisted on carrying John's heavy drum to the door at the end of each class and giving us enormous hugs. After a while it seemed unimaginable that this affectionate, child-like lady had once frightened us.

We made music with these ladies. We marched, walked, held parades, waltzed, or simply sat and rocked back and forth in our chairs as many of them did. We generally tried to find what was pleasurable and meaningful to them, and when we did, no matter how simple the activity was, it also became truly pleasurable and meaningful to us.

We Meet Roger

In another class we met Roger. He was dressed in baggy gray wash pants and shirt. His head was down, the typical stance of so many in the institution. We discovered that he had been in the alcoholic ward for 10 years. Formerly he had been a tap dancer in clubs all over the Boston area. We asked Roger to dance, with John filling in a bass line on his drums.

With the critical ear of the drummer, John was surprised by the rhythms coming from Roger's feet. The steps were intricate and unpredictable, steps reminiscent of Bojangles, the Nicholas Brothers, and Sandman Simms from a time when tap dance was experiencing its greatest popularity.

Part of the Arts and the Aging plan was to create a touring show of entertainment by older people with arts skills. We mentioned to our program director the possibility of having Roger perform at a senior lunch site. She had strong reservations about using a patient from a mental institution. However, after a trial visit by Roger at one site she agreed to his coming regularly. Later, she even aspired to get him on the payroll as a performer.

We were so naive about institutions that we didn't know how unrealistic it was to daydream about Roger dancing in fancy clothes, performing again as he once did in clubs; Roger having his own apartment again; Roger leading a real life once more.

After working together for a number of months, we inquired about getting Roger out of the hospital. We found out that after 10 years there are in-between steps such as half-way houses. A patient doesn't just leave an institution and get an apartment. We were warned also that few people make it "outside" after a long stay in the hospital. Roger's social worker, with an overload of cases, didn't know Roger was a dancer. He was very helpful when we talked to him. Within a week after our request, Roger was moved to a half-way house.

From there, Roger went back to his Narragansett Indian community in South County, and to its senior citizen club activities. He has his own apartment now, 5 1/2 years later. He continues with our show which has traveled to nursing homes, lunch sites, prisons, schools, housing projects, parks, and even vacant lots. It has been exciting not only to watch Roger recall his old tricks as his dancing becomes clearer, louder, and livelier, but also to watch his independence return.

In the beginning we picked him up for every show. Now he will take a bus halfway across the state to meet us. If the bus from downtown is late, he will walk the mile to my house. And he walks quickly. Last summer when we were hauling a portable stage he surprised us by pitching in and lifting equipment right along with us. He treated us all to lemonade after the show, and over the holidays he gave us each an Indian beaded tie to wear for performances. These changes are dramatic and they began in an institution where "change" is not a common word, and at an age when "people don't change."

Natural Creativity

Although few patients have been professional artists, we are often struck by the talent among patients in general. Sometimes they create with the direct, free, bold approach of a child. Other times, the complexity of their life experiences reveals expressions of personal history and fantasy all in one.

We are accustomed now to a kind of poetry spoken in the wards. During one dance class, we were moving our arms up and down and I thought Helen was saying, "like a bird." But when I came closer, she was really saying, "like a bride running to her husband!"

Jean from K Building said to me one day, "The wind makes the colors in the sky. I taught you, now you must teach me." There are people who have lines that they repeat time after time. "My name is Betty. My husband left me after the war. The hell with him." "Bondy," a lady in her nineties told me, "I'm a Boston baked bean. Give me 13 dandelions for my grave. Roses are too expensive." And there was the small Frenchman who would continually ask, "Will I be cured? Will I be happy?"

Art programs encourage these expressions, allow a time for them to happen, media for them to happen through, space for them to be arranged, rearranged, expanded or modified, and present an ear, an audience.

Even in the locked ward there is hope, and through art, change is possible. When we went to RA.4, we saw a large room with two long rows of chairs on which men sat looking off into space. A television was on but no one was watching it. A few men paced back and forth. No one spoke. Our first "conversations" with these men were wordless. We volleyed a ballon to them. Soon almost everyone began to hit it back to us. We sat next to them with a drum and asked each to hit it. We tossed a bean bag around and played music. We squatted on the floor and offered each one a marker and paper to write on.

The first move to return the volley, the first bang on the drum, the first mark on the paper gave us information about these men. No matter how "institutionalized" they had become, locked in a ward in lethargy, dullness, and obedience, each of them still revealed a unique personality. Through music, movement, drawing, and writing we were getting to know each other.

Transformations

Rick had been there probably longer than anyone. He would hit the drum hard and when he drew he would use long, parallel strokes, sometimes drawn with such force that the paper would tear. When Hal drew, he floated little lines on the paper and then crossed them till the paper was filled with X's. His drum playing was light, also, and if you shook his hand, it was so soft you would have to prompt him to squeeze.

John and I would set up our chairs at opposite ends of the long rectangle of men and try to modify the group into a circular form. John would play the drums at one end and I would lead movement from mine. The moves had to be kept simple and we might do one move for 10 minutes at a time. We began chanting as we lifted our arms up and down, "Up, up, up, up," and "Down, down, down, down." A third of the men were participating on and off. Some would forget and just leave their arms up in the air; some would need to be called by name because they would fall back into their dreams, but even this was progress compared to the first weeks.

As the sessions went on, we introduced time for solo dances. Different men would take turns in the center of the floor playing and dancing with a tamborine while John played the drums. Bobby, who spoke no more than a "yes" or "no" if you tried to talk with him, would take long solos. He became almost totally transformed; brightening up, raising his head, and stepping lightly. As we continued over the weeks, more and more men were willing to take a turn and many days we were surprised by a burst of spirit from a man who was ordinarily withdrawn.

We also set up tables for drawing. This was usually after moving and making music. At first we had to bring the drawing materials over to Hal where he was lying or squatting on the floor. After a few weeks we were able to get him to come over to the table. Hal is sixty-six and has been at the medical center since he was fourteen. His records say he was a bright boy who loved to read. He was brought to the hospital because he was hearing voices. In his latest medical report he was described by the doctor as "100 percent uncommunicative" and "mute." No one had heard him talk except when he hallucinated. He compressed his lips tightly when asked a question.

It was at the drawing table that we discovered Hal was rational, and even romantic, and quite willing to communicate— but in his own unique way. While the other men drew, Hal preferred to write. He would write phrases like "great scott," "Gullivers Travels." or the names of birds. We brought in a bird chart, and for the first time we heard his voice "Thrush!—Jay, a bluejay." Eventually he would read off the names of all the birds clearly. I began writing words next to his words to stimulate him more. Sometimes he would copy the word, sometimes write the opposite word, or sometimes make a slogan. For instance, I wrote "hard" and he wrote "It's hard to beat Skippy." I wrote "fight," and he wrote "tuberculosis." Then I began writing parts of sentences that he might finish. "I wish I could . . ." He added "see a poem lovelier than a tree."

I wrote "I wish I were . . ." Hal added "dead."
"My favorite color is . . ." He added "black."
"Black is the color of . . ." He added, "screech owl."
"I want to be . . ." He added, "free."
"Dear mother . . ." He added "I love you."

One day an attendant came in a bit drunk and was creating a disruption in our class. We looked down at Hal's paper; he had written "this man is?" We all cracked up laughing.

Hal will not only read things aloud now, but he is answering more and more. Since we have been writing together the nurse in charge has also taken an interest in him and brings him to the canteen for ice cream. She is delighted when she asks him to tell us where they went, and what kind of ice cream he had, and he answers. We notice the attendant on the floor gives him a special invitation to go down to bingo and offers to help him play. We continue to write our poems together. This is one we wrote recently. I tried to follow his lead. We each used a different color marker.

The best literature is written by *a baby*
The child knows *heaven*
I sit by the brook and think of *you*
I wait for the monarch butterfly to *fly*
I look at the moon and the *shepherd and the sheep*
I feel the wind and wish for *the lover*
My heart is *broke*
I cannot find my *lover*
I watch the sheep and console myself with *soda.*

Toward the end of the drawing time, John takes a few of the men off to a corner to play the drums. They sit in a small circle with the drum between them. They take turns hitting it or at times all play it together. Initially Phil would play the drum with one hand, striking it with his hand cupped—just a steady beating. Phil's playing has progressed through a number of stages—from playing with one cupped hand to two hands playing simultaneously; to two hands alternately (more sophisticated and difficult for many mental patients); to playing with two hands alternately, the hands flattened so that the palm strikes the drum in a more controlled, forceful fashion. Originally, if John asked Phil to strike the drum the same number of times he did, Phil could not do it. Now he can, most of the time. John gets Phil to imitate things he does on the drum after they have had their free exchange. He is capable of doing this quite well and picking up on the subtleties which show he is concentrating and aware.

Kinesthetic Rewards

It is impossible to separate the pleasures in making art, music, dance, and words. There is a lot of overlapping. When the men are playing the drum, as well as enjoying their sounds they are enjoying the feel of the drum skin and the movement of the hands and wrists coordinating themselves on top of the drum. When they are working with clay, the hands are again moving—going through a whole gamut of possibilities, twisting, squeezing, poking, pulling. When they move the hands to music or squeeze and throw a foam rubber ball around, they are also enjoying the sound of the music, and the shapes the hands and ball are drawing in the air. The enjoyment of all this hand movement can have a practical side; the hand-eye coordination and flexibility developed can increase some of the skills now lacking, like tying shoes, shaving, buttoning shirts.

Overcoming Small Budgets

Working in institutions for five-and-a-half years we have also learned to tackle other practical problems. We have found ways to overcome small budgets. John has discovered that metal dustpans make wonderful gongs and has collected different tone dustpans from a number of places where we have worked—with permission, of course. When we ran out of drawing paper, we discovered the rolls of paper for the doctor's examining table. Also, paper towels and cups seem abundant and can be drawn on and decorated.

This summer we discovered that kitchens of institutions can offer materials when there is no more money left for art supplies. We used a large pan of dried beans that made a pleasurable, sensual experience when we sifted them through our fingers. We have yet to request salt and flour from the kitchen for a good self-hardening clay, but that's next. Large hospitals often have their own wood shop too, and different shaped odds and ends of wood make good blocks. Some of the men enjoy sanding the blocks, which incorporates movement, sound, sight, smell, touch, and the satisfaction of turning something rough into something smooth. George made a cross with the blocks and then placed other blocks around it.

"That's St. Lucia and Martha," he explained. I thought, the Martha of the biblical Mary and Martha, but he added "Raye." Then he pointed to "Betty Grable and Errol Flynn" next to the cross.

"What are they saying?" I asked.
"They're singing *Buttons and Bows.*"
We sang *Buttons and Bows* together.

Fantasy World and Reality

Many of the men have opened up a great deal. We have shared openly with them in ways we sometimes don't achieve even with close friends. The mundane matters that usually concern us are put aside and we partake of rich fantasy worlds. Even in a fantasy world there is organizing, decision making, and reality.

Gerald Communicates

A striking visual example of this is a series of drawings made by Gerald. He never spoke but always took part in the movement session. Then he would draw or, rather, scribble for the rest of the time. After 6 months, I heard an attendant standing behind him say, "That's a nice horse, Gerald." I did a double-take because Gerald had never drawn any recognizable form. There on his paper was a horse! And even more striking, we looked at his older pictures which were still hanging on the wall. The vague shape of a horse with a saddle, generous mane and tail were forming, as if making its way out of a cocoon, becoming more recognizable with each drawing till this day when the horse emerged (Figure 1-4).

Art Programs Can Revive Human Spirit

Age, obviously, is not the barrier to growth, change and healing. The older age may be the very reason that healing can take place. The body naturally heals itself. "Time heals." "He's gotten mellow in his old age." It is very possible that older persons in an institution can overcome their problems and return again to a life. For a population so institutionalized and so neglected, these people still have potential spirit, life, and humor. Art programs can offer ways to uncover and revive these qualities. As Hal said laughingly to us one day: "My cheeks are rosy anyway; I can't be dead!"

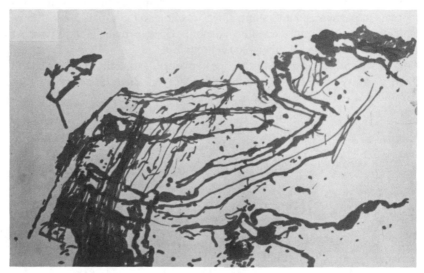

1

2

3

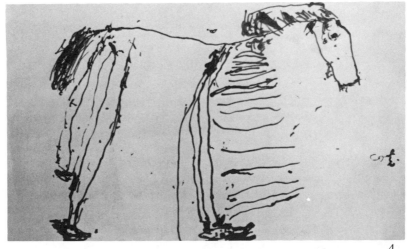

4

SUGGESTED READINGS

Bertherat, T., & Bernstein, C. *The body has its reasons: Anti-exercises and self-awareness*. New York: Avon Books, 1976.

Greefeld, J. *A child called noah*. New York: Pocket Books, 1970.

Höper, C., Kutzleb, U., Stobbe, A., & Weber, B. *Awareness games*. Personal growth through group interaction. New York: St. Martins Press, 1974.

Pesso, A. *Movement in psychotherapy*. Psychomotor techniques and training. New York: New York University Press, 1969.

Polster, E., & Polster, M. *Gestalt therapy integrated: Contours of theory & practice*. New York: Vintage Books, 1973.

PART IV

SIGNIFICANT RESOURCES: A PSYCHOLOGIST AND A POET

Implicit in the writings of all our contributors is a profound belief in the creative process. So closely allied with play and spontaneity, creative process is different from imitation and all that is associated with meaningless busy-work. It has to do with the innermost cravings of the human spirit, the anima, to express often unreleased, unheard feelings kept captive since childhood.

Creative arts practitioners who work with older groups sometimes encounter resistance to activities that may at first seem childlike, that help release long-protected inhibitions. For this reason, it is important to know the leader/facilitator role well and the subtleties of group interaction. Only then is it possible effectively to guide individuals-in-group to paths of self-discovery and growth.

For this section of our book we have invited two professionals to share their unique, but harmonious, views on creative process, the role of leader and the evolution of the group.

Marilyn Barsky is a clinical psychologist whose own work has led her to incorporate many of the techniques of the creative arts with her clients. Highlighting some of the pitfalls in the way of reaching individuals in a rehabilitative group, she delineates the personal qualities and skills desirable in an effective leader.

Marc Kaminsky is a poet and educator who suggests in the following passages from an essay that the concerns of group work lie within the sphere of interest of writers and other arts leaders. He illuminates distinct phases in the emergence of a group. Then, using metaphor and other poetic prose, he describes ways in which the creative artist/leader encourages individuation-within-community.

*Creative arts workers can learn to utilize their own
innate creativity for the benefit of the senior citizens
they work with and for the enhancement of their
creative powers*

**Marilyn Barsky, Ed.D. Clinical Psychologist: American Board of Professional Psychology
Diplomate;** is in private practice of family, group, and individual therapy in New Jersey. She
uses creative drama techniques in group work with all ages. Dr. Barsky has been a nursing home
consultant. She is the author of several articles in professional journals and is at work on a novel.

THE CREATIVE POWERS WITHIN US
A PHILOSOPHY AND RATIONALE

by Marilyn Barsky

A bird does not sing because he has an answer; he
sings because he has a song.

Chinese proverb

Anyone who has worked with the aged in a nursing home knows how little it
takes to bring a light into the eyes of a burned-out old man or woman. I firmly
believe that even a simple, loving smile, a squeeze of the hand, or a light pat
on the shoulder can help to retard the effects of physical deterioration or
organic brain syndrome. How well I remember one old gentleman who,
though I saw him weekly, could never remember my name. Yet he knew my
face and his own face lit up whenever he saw me. He would recite poetry
learned in early childhood, and accurately too. We used to sit on his bed and
recite poetry like *Barbara Fritchie*, or sing songs like *Molly Malone* and
When Irish Eyes Are Smiling. This man came alive during our hours together
through his songs and poems.

My main intention was to help him have a meaningful interpersonal exchange with another human being, to keep him in contact with reality, to
stimulate his memory and one or more of the five senses so that deterioration,
physical and psychological, would be, at the least, slowed down. And I
wanted to reconnect him with a sense of imaginative play, by means of his
remembered songs and poems.

Let's Pretend . . .

"Let's pretend . . ." Remember how often that phrase was used among us when we were kids? For many of us, it is only when we are children that we indulge in such imaginative pursuits. Except for professional and amateur creative artists, adulthood often means the suppression of the deepest need of the human spirit for rejuvenation through the use of the imagination and creative pursuits. Yet at every age from the cradle to senescence, there is the need to utilize the creative powers that lie within all of us if we could only find a sure way to tap them.

The nineteenth-century English poet Samuel T. Coleridge called the imagination "that willing suspension of disbelief that constitutes poetic faith." The Freudians think of creativity as "regression in the service of the ego," believing that our creative powers come directly out of the unconscious, or, in other words, from our childhood wishes, dreams, and fantasies, not yet suppressed for the sake of the "reality principle."

In a society in which the Puritan ethic has been the predominant mode for the typical adult, the pleasure principle is often relegated to an inferior position. For many of us, an early connection has been made between the pleasure principle and creativity. To our detriment, we are bidden to put away childish toys in adulthood, and by doing so are often barred from the use of our fullest, active creative powers. What price maturity!

Creative Stimulation and Survival

Yet for the child, creative play *is* work, the stuff through which he or she tries on roles and rehearses for maturity. But creative stimulation for the infant and child is much more than that. Mental health workers like John Bowlby, Réne Spitz, William Goldfarb, and others long ago demonstrated how lack of sensory and affective stimulation in infancy can often lead to stunted intellects, warped personalities, and even to "marasmus" and death.

When the adult grows older, retires, and no longer can participate in the mainstream of American society, he or she may often also be cut off from important sources of affective and sensory stimulation. Is it too far-fetched to state that when this happens to the senior citizen in our society, the person, like the deprived infant, can shrivel up, deteriorate, develop the adult equivalent of marasmus, and die? There is ample evidence that just such sequelae are the rule for many elderly people in our society.

Only very recently has society begun to pay attention to its elderly, and to acknowledge its debt and obligation to them. We are now seeing a proliferation of day-care centers for senior citizens, of nursing homes for long-term care, golden age programs, and geriatric activities. For the first time in American history, many kinds of personnel are being hired or are serving as volunteers to implement creative types of programs for this population in the community and in institutions.

Senior citizens share human needs in common with all other groups and in addition have some unique needs. Like the rest of us, senior citizens need continuing physical, mental, and emotional stimulation; affection, approval, recognition, a feeling of self-worth.

Uniquely, older persons are experiencing decline in their physical prowess, often a decrement of their mental powers, and quite typically, personality tendencies to withdraw from others which become exacerbated and overt. At the very time when these internal events are inevitably occurring to older citizens, their middle-aged children may tend to push them aside, and sometimes they must even uproot and place them in impersonal homes. This phenomenon occurs both because of the inevitable new pressures on the middle-aged, and because of the prevailing attitude in our society that "the old don't count." For this age group, then, creative outlets are tantamount to survival.

It cannot be emphasized too strongly, however, that by creative outlets, I do not mean the perfunctory and token programs, too often seen in nursing home facilities, in which prefabricated, stereotypical, and uninspired arts and crafts programs are presented to senior citizens; for example, paint-by-number kits or the copying of magazine pictures. Authentic creativity means, rather, the expression of one's innermost, highly individual experiences through whatever media is natural.

Creativity: Reciprocal and Transactional

Senior citizens, like all groups in the population, come in all shapes and sizes. The rates and qualities of the aging process are different for each person, as are the talents, backgrounds, perceptions, and inner lives. The task of the creative arts worker is to encourage and nurture that which is already there and only needs awakening or reawakening.

Creative arts workers can learn to utilize their own innate creativity for the benefit of the senior citizens they work with, and incidentally, for the enhancement of their own creative powers. Creativity, in this context, is reciprocal and functions in the interpersonal field to enhance both the geriatric worker and the elderly individual. Creativity, in this sense, is transactional. An important result of the use of creative arts methodology is the development of the capacity for positive relating with others.

Desirable Traits: Creative Arts Therapists and Leaders

How do workers tap their own creative powers for enhancing the life of the senior citizens? In addition to the special training they have, and the talents they bring to their own particular creative endeavors, whether it be dance, art, music, or drama, to work successfully with old people they must develop certain other assets and personality traits.

First, and perhaps foremost, workers must *like* old people. They must enjoy association with the elderly, for as with small children, older citizens are very sensitive to nuances in demeanor and nonverbal cues of all kinds in others. They know well enough when a smile is forced, or a pat on the hand perfunctory. Workers must have or attempt to cultivate what psychotherapists call "accurate empathy." For the lucky few, this trait is inborn; for others, it must be carefully cultivated and honed. It is sometimes helpful and comforting to discuss thorny problems with colleagues and sympathetic supervisory staff.

Workers must possess enough personal self-esteem and inner resources that they can accept the fact that the appearance and behaviors of more than a few older people (like younger people!) can be quite unappealing. But, as a psychologist working with all kinds of people, I have often been surprised to discover that the least likely people can become attractive to us as we understand them better. And if we succeed, at last, in helping them, they can become beautiful.

Arts workers will find that some elderly people will be difficult to involve in any organized activity. With some, it will take all one's ingenuity, wit, and charm to engage them even slightly. And, no matter how persistent and resourceful the workers are, some they will fail to involve at all. For these moments of truth, it is imperative that each worker has stored up confidence enough to take in stride such blows to the self-esteem.

It is most important that these workers enjoy people in general, and find satisfaction in relating to others. In many nursing homes and other institutional settings, workers will face resistances, albeit subtle, from many sides. They may have to win over skeptical, even hostile administrators, as well as nurses, aides, and other day-to-day caregivers. It is amazing how many residents in a facility cannot be found on any particular day if just one nurse takes a dislike for a worker, or does not comprehend the purpose of the program!

Overall, creative arts workers must be:

spontaneous and open to their own feelings and to those of others. They will need to use their openness to cut through layers of resistance and defense, as well as to tap their inner resources and wellsprings of creative energies.

flexible, coming to their task with a wide repertoire of techniques and strategies to gain maximum involvement.

calm, collected, and well-organized. A temperamental personality is not an asset, but verve and energy are musts.

persistent, with great patience. The satisfaction felt if there is even one success with one elderly person is enough to compensate for less successful moments. If one senior citizen can become more open, more alive, and more feeling through utilizing the imagination and creative powers, something valuable will have been attained.

Creative Goals and Methodologies

As a consultant psychologist in a long-term county nursing facility, I ran a weekly group where I attempted a variety of creative approaches. For a group therapist or counselor, there are two kinds of groups. The first, a traditional therapy group, is essentially rehabilitative, with a major focus upon obtaining certain personality changes for individuals within it. The second kind I would call "inspirational," in which the focus is on infusing the individual with spirit or zest for life.

While the aim of a rehabilitation group is to liberate individuals from the bondage of their own hang-ups and self-destructive life-styles, the goal of a group in a long-term nursing facility is to help individuals adjust to current realities. Yet, in a very true sense, they can be liberated *in spirit.* They can be helped to lift themselves out of the doldrums and to find creative powers in themselves either for the first time, or to rediscover them.

In the particular group that I will describe this was precisely the mission, and to this end certain creative methodologies were introduced.

The group consisted of senior citizens in the nursing home primarily because they were too incapacitated to be taken care of elsewhere; and a number of young, severely handicapped adults who supposedly could not function outside this highly protective setting. The rationale for mixing the two categories was simple. One subgroup could serve as catalytic agent for the other. The wisdom and experience of the elderly could be a valuable assist to the young, while the enthusiasm and zest of the latter could fuel the spirits of the elderly. On a dynamic level, the participants could serve as surrogate parents and children for each other.

As the group facilitator, my goals for the members of this group were:

to increase *self-awareness,* by helping each member to clarify inner feelings, goals, strengths and weaknesses, needs, and fears;

to increase *interpersonal skills,* by assisting each individual in the group to develop a greater capacity for trusting each other, for increasing self-disclosure, as well as increasing ability to listen and empathize with others; to develop increased awareness of other people's feelings and needs and temperamental difficulties.

to help members clarify their *value systems,* by sorting out their philosophy of life; providing the opportunity to discuss, in an open atmosphere, death and dying and its significance for each person as well as other kinds of spiritual concerns.

to promote *sensory awakening,* an awareness of one's body, its movement and rhythm; to stimulate sight, sound, touch, and smell.

to develop *spontaneity,* through a sense of playfulness and participation in song, dance, role-play, guided fantasy, use of dreams, imagery, poetry, and story.

Let me emphasize that these were *ideal* goals for the group, and of course, in reality, the group fell far short of reaching all these aims.

It consisted of nine individuals, three of them under fifty years old. Incidentally, the attendance throughout the program was close to perfect, due both to the enthusiasm of the members themselves and also to excellent cooperation from administration, nurses, and aides.

An ultimate goal of a creative worker who deals with the elderly is to encourage senior citizens to get along without the intervention of a professional. In other words, we want them to seek and find what they need and want from other seniors and, when possible, from friends and relatives in their environment. This is a way to remain vibrant and alive, giving and receiving creative solace and nurturance until the very moment of death.

I remember a beautiful eighty-five year-old woman who came into the nursing home against her will with all her faculties intact. She had been placed there by a relative who no longer was able to care for her. She was in a deep depression when I first began to work with her, feeling not only a sense of loss, but one of betrayal and abandonment. The most crucial part of my task was to teach her to reach out to those around her, to those who wanted and needed a relationship with a caring, loving, still very vital person. When she began to take an interest in and to seek out those residents who were less fortunate physically and mentally than she, I knew that my job was done. She adjusted to the home and found a new purpose in living. She then became her own therapist. At the same time, like Grandma Moses, she found a new profession in her old age—that of a "therapist" for others!

Role Play

One technique successfully used with this group was role play. Naturally, the use of any technique of this kind must be postponed until the group members have learned to be comfortable both with the therapist and with each other. It must wait, also, until there is group cohesiveness and trust. In addition, any technique used must arise out of the spontaneous discussion and needs of the group. This can be described as a "spontaneous event."

One example occurred in the following manner. The group session began with glum silence. There seemed to be a great deal of covert discontent displayed in the demeanor and countenances of the various members of the group. A latecomer, a twenty-five year-old quadraplegic woman, had zoomed into the room in her electric wheelchair, her rather jerky and hyperactive movements and facial expression suggesting actual fury.

I waited patiently for some member of the group to open the discussion. Finally, the quadraplegic opened, "I'm so dammed pissed!" she said. Gradually, other group members elicited the reasons. A seventy-year-old woman in a wheelchair who often played the role of surrogate mother coaxed the younger woman to tell her problem. The young woman exploded about the rehabilitation nurse who was threatening to take away her electric wheelchair and replace it with a manual one in order to "give me more exercise." Several other group members empathized with her because they, too, had experienced difficulties with this particular nurse. Now some other members in wheelchairs, both old and young, joined in with angry accusations about this worker's "cruelty."

After allowing the members to ventilate feelings for a time, I suggested that we do some role play, with the quadraplegic playing herself having a conversation with the rehab nurse, played by the seventy-year-old woman. I set up the scene.

The first time around, both were somewhat self-conscious and stilted. We then switched roles, using the same scenario. Gradually, others were brought into the scene to play different roles and bring their own ideas as well as their own unique and individual feelings to their parts. On one occasion, when I felt that a member could not express what he was really thinking and feeling, I used a psychodramatic technique called doubling. I stood behind the person and voiced what I thought he was really feeling and thinking, in terms of my estimate of his core problems.

By the end of the one and one-half hour session, the results were gratifying. Not only did self-consciousness and reluctance abate remarkably, but also the whole tenor of the session changed to a less angry, more jocular and humorous tone. A great deal of anger and frustration had dissipated, not only concerning the rehab nurse, but also about other frustrating issues in the nursing home between various workers and residents.

In addition, through identification, the residents began to get in touch with other, more positive, motives of the workers. They discovered that distance and a sense of humor are effective antidotes to anger and despair. Finally, this first attempt at role play led to others when this technique seemed to be the most efficacious and meaningful route to deal with day-to-day issues. Thus role play can be utilized both for assertiveness training and for rehearsal of real-life situations. A fringe benefit of such creative manuevers is that a group becomes closer, more cohesive, and more trusting of each other.

Guided Imagery

Relaxation with imagery was another successful strategy used with this group. This standard induction technique consists of promoting progressive relaxation starting with the muscles of the head, neck, and shoulders, and progressing downward to the legs, feet, and toes. Seven of the nine members of the group became deeply relaxed. The two members who did not attain a relaxed state quietly watched the procedure and were quite fascinated by it.

While the group members were in this relaxed condition, I suggested that they imagine themselves in a lovely green forest, that they try to see themselves in their mind's eye walking along a path on a crisp, sunny autumn day, smelling the aroma of pines. "Visualize the beautiful orange, yellow, and red leaves of the trees; notice the vivid colors of the fall flowers," I said. Imagine yourselves bending over to pick the flowers. Feel the soft velvety stems and buds in your fingers. Hear the laughter of young children running through the woods, and the birds singing." (The group leader was scolded by several members for encouraging the group to pick the flowers in the forest!)

The rationale for using this methodology is to train the members in deep relaxation and to heighten sensory stimulation by the use of imagery. Later, I encouraged members to induce their own fantasies and to use the particular imagery that gave them the most pleasure and relaxation in order to encourage their own innate creative powers.

Other techniques I used came from the encounter movement. Group exercises were initiated in which members were asked to sit back, close their eyes, and imagine a layered ball with an inner core, a middle and outer layer. I asked them to describe it to themselves. Each member, in turn, was asked to tell the group what he and she had fantasized. In rehabilitative groups, such an exercise is used to help individuals deal with character armor and then to look deeper into the ball to find the "core" self.

In other words, the ball is a symbol for the self. For example, a person who visualizes a hard outer core with an inner core that is soft as a marshmallow can be hypothesized on a dynamic level as being a person who is covering up considerable vulnerability. In this group, however, the technique was used more for the purpose of inspiring some creative types of fantasy. One old gentleman fantasized a white steel cruise ship that had three layers. In the outer layer, hanging over the side, there were lifeboats. When we talked about it, he confided that he always wanted to travel around the world on a tramp steamer.

At another time I asked the group members to close their eyes, and to try to remember themselves at a particular age such as six, twelve, or twenty-five, and then to report their remembrances to the group in as vivid a way as possible. This caused some rather deep psychological material to emerge from a few members. I particularly remember the seventy-year-old woman who ventilated angry feelings harbored towards her long-departed mother, which she had suppressed until the current disclosure. She reported to me later, in private, just how liberating it was to talk about her feelings in a non-judgmental, sympathetic atmosphere.

An art therapist might try such a technique through the utilization of members' drawings of themselves at various ages, then have them show the result to the group. Acting out and/or drawing the dreams of individual members is another useful technique for eliciting interesting material.

Death and Dying

Another encounter-type technique was to ask each member what they would do if they found out they had only 6 months to live and had just inherited $10 thousand. For older people, particularly, this exercise can stimulate discussion about death and dying, topics about which most people are ambivalent. Though we long to be able to open up and discuss this sensitive issue, we are constrained by old taboos and superstitions. It is helpful, particularly for senior citizens, if they can be encouarged to talk openly with each other about such matters. A word of caution is in order, however. The safest measure is to wait for a group member to initiate the discussion of death and dying. But if you are going to use this technique be very sure that you know each group member well, that group members know and like each other well and are comfortable and nondefensive.

Autobiography

The group members were encouraged, also, to use a tape recorder between sessions, in order to record their life stories. This autobiographical technique had only limited success with this particular group. Another similar method is to encourage group members to keep a journal, writing in it for a few minutes every day. This works, of course, only for those individuals who can still write. Many older people have stopped writing altogether because of crippling arthritis. If some of these people can be induced to do some writing, it not only can stimulate their creativity, but may also help to reduce crippling of the fingers and hands.

These are only some of the techniques I used with this group. The number of methodologies for group or individual work are virtually endless, limited only by the goals, motivation, creativity, and particular training of the worker or volunteer.

The Importance of Creative Transactions in the Interpersonal Field

It must be emphasized that creative approaches are used mainly to facilitate process, not to bring about product. Certainly the most important outcomes of the creative process in geriatric settings are the enhancement of intrapersonal vibrancy and joy, and more positive and rewarding interpersonal relationships between the older people, between workers and the older people, and with family members and friends.

Awakening a person to the life that is still burning within, to the surrounding environment, and to people whom he or she can love and be loved by in return—all of this represents the strongest rationale for the creative process as an approach by a geriatric therapist and a creative arts leader. Both of us are encouraging the senior citizen to take risk, to reach out to others and to receive in turn.

Make no mistake, this is not an easy way to work. By their very reluctance and recalcitrance, the aged tax and stretch us to employ our fullest inner resources and creative powers. The pitfalls may be many, but the benefits of working this way are worth all we can bring to it. For both of us are, in essence, working with the elderly to recreate the life wish.

SUGGESTED READINGS

Blatner, H. *Acting in.* New York: Springer Publishing Co., 1973.

Kagan, J., (Ed.). *Creativity and learning.* Boston: Beacon Press, 1967.

Koberg, D., & Bagnall, J. *The universal traveler—A soft-systems guide to: Creativity, problem-solving and the process of reaching goals.* Los Altos, California: William Kaufmann, Inc., 1974.

McNiff, S. *The arts and psychotherapy.* Springfield, Illinois: Charles C. Thomas, Inc., 1981.

Otto, H.A., *Group methods to actualize human potential.* Beverly Hills, California: The Holistic Press, 1970.

Robey, H. *There's a dance in the old dame yet.* Boston, Mass.: Little, Brown & Company, 1982.

Stein, M. *Stimulating creativity.* (Vols. I & II). New York: Academic Press, Inc., 1975.

Each one wants a world larger than his or her own skin to live in. It is only through working on a project larger than one's individual existence that one becomes fully human. The group allows people . . . a place in which to taste the joy of generating a sense of community, of coming together, raising an emotional roofbeam and four walls, and going on, more complete in themselves for having built with others.

Marc Kaminsky, M.A. Summa Cum Laude; M.S.W. Hunter College School of Social Work; teaches literature and poetry workshops at Hunter College. Founder and Director of the Artists and Elders Project of the Teachers and Writers Collaborative, he is also Director of the West Side Senior Center, Jewish Association of Services for the Aged. Mr. Kaminsky is the author of *What's Inside You It Shines Out of You,* Horizon, 1974; three books of poetry, numerous poems and essays, and a new collection of poems, *Daily Bread.* He is Co-director of the Brookdale Institute of Humanities, Arts and Aging, of Hunter College.

INVOCATIONS
OF GROUP PROCESS
AND LEADERSHIP
by Marc Kaminsky

Introduction

In these excerpts from an essay included in ALL THAT OUR EYES
HAVE WITNESSED *(Horizon Press, 1982) Mr. Kaminsky is preparing a group of poets and writers to teach in the Artists and Elders Project.* All are proficient in their art; all are interested in aging and in
working with older adults. None of them, however, has much use for
group work. Yet their workshops will involve small groups of older
people.*

*As a first step, he engages them in a discussion of their own ex-
periences within all kinds of groups.*

Groups are always an encounter with the unknown and surely no one can plan
or foresee what comes next. That is what makes groups the miraculous things
they sometimes become. No matter how many times people in a group have
surprised you, shocked you, filled you with amazement, with profound
respect; no matter how often you have come away with a heightened faith that

---

* A joint venture of Teachers and Writers Collaborative and Brookdale Center
on Aging, Institute on Humanities, Arts, and Aging, Hunter College.

group process can call forth unexpected powers, you never get to be on familiar terms with the unexpected. How often the energies of ordinary people assume miraculous shapes. And if the people in the group are in touch with the unconscious, if they are artists, or a workshop of old people writing poetry, truly incredible things can happen.

The First Phase

Wise leaders tolerate the paradoxical nature of this First Phase. People are anxious and confused. The leader allows distance and provides structure; promotes but safeguards against intimacy. People are ambivalent about getting involved, and the leader allows everyone to have it both ways.

In the First Phase, a "nondefinitive definition" of the group's reasons for coming together must be clearly agreed on. Like everything else, this will change, and so it must be left open to change. It must be clear, and yet its clarity must not be a mode of rigidity. Built into this early statement of purpose should be the seeds of its transformation into something else which will itself be left open to include the not-yet-known.

So this is the task of the first time or times together: to build an answer to the question, "What am I doing here?" Or, "What is it all about?" What projects or goals make connections among people in the room and open their lives out towards some common future? Passengers sharing the same compartment at the beginning of a journey, on discovering that they share the same destination, often start exchanging stories of their lives and recount by what crooked roads and byways they came to be in the same place, heading in the same direction. The group, then, can recreate this age-old experience, these openings of the heart in the course of a journey.

Wise leaders, knowing the natural pull toward this solidarity of travelers, do not push things, or rush them. They put their cards on the table while allowing others to keep theirs hidden. They are open-handed; they show they have nothing up their sleeves—no magical power, no secret purpose.

Purpose

The group will be what the people in the group make it. The cards the leader turns over in an attempt to piece together a royal house in which they can spend some time together, are a range of purposes, a starting place for the group to freely trade ideas until a shared sense of purpose begins to emerge.

In group-work theory, this declaration of a way of being together is called a contract. In the group, as in the society of which it is a part, people are afraid of being cheated, made fools of, sucked in. The contract is a way of creating trust.

The trust-work that goes on at the beginning of a group is at the heart of everything you say and do. This is the heart of the matter: to create trust in a situation in which people distrust each other. That early statement of purpose which comprehends the wishes and aims of everyone in the room is the acknowledgement of a bond among people walking the same road for a while. To that journey, each one brings a capacity to trust that has, one hopes, never quite been killed off; if it has, life is unendurable. Walt Whitman once said that whoever walks a mile without sympathy walks to his own grave.

To the group, each one brings years of wandering in unfriendly cities and a desire to walk in sympathy with others. The wish for solidarity, frustrated by the way society is organized, may be timid in showing itself. It is nonetheless there, seeking its occasion, waiting for a situation in which its trust will not be betrayed. Each one knows this already, even if it is known only as the absence of something, a kind of hunger which as yet has no name.

Each one wants a world larger than his or her own skin to live in. It is only through working on a project larger than one's individual existence that one becomes fully human. The group allows people who feel that they have "no place to be somebody" a place in which to taste the joy of generating a sense of community, of coming together, raising an emotional roofbeam and four walls, and going on, more complete in themselves for having built with others.

In this First Phase, wise leaders must actively create a sense of large possibility. They must inspire others without diminishing their capacity to take charge. In short, the leader must provide the table and the chairs but not the room arrangement; that will arise from the pushes and pulls of the people who shift things about as they make a place for themselves in the room. In the beginning, the leader will provide the coffee and cake, but will also welcome whatever anyone else brings to the table, so that the offerings will keep coming in and grow abundant, and the group will one day become a banquet.

Phase Two

Conflict

In Phase Two, trouble begins. Here, the pecking order is slowly becoming visible amid a whirr of flying feathers, accompanied by a lot of squawking and—among the less active combatants—ruffled feathers. Member against member, group against leader—the strain is felt everywhere; the struggle occasionally breaks out into open conflict, then grows diffuse again. The members are fighting each other for status. The group is fighting the leader for power. At bottom, each one is fighting not to be diminished. What to do?

The wise leader, expecting trouble, is not alarmed, welcomes conflict for the good things it carries with it. Energy, wit, self-assertion, pride, anger, criticism—these things enliven a group and a person. Old people who at first glance seemed sleepy, after a few pecks, look "perky"—as I heard one old woman say. It is like the horseradish that I once saw another old woman swallow a spoonful of, in one gulp. A flood of tears came to her eyes, horseradish tears. I asked, "Why do you do this?" She said, "I'm ninety-four. How else can I feel I'm still alive?" She sighed with pleasure; it was the pleasure of feeling something keenly.

Conflict is not horseradish, but it does have value in bringing out the fullness of each person's particular flavor. "Without contraries is no progression," runs one of Blake's proverbs.

Without Conflict the People in the Group Cannot Take Power

So conflict is the native element of the group at this time. Do not seek to avoid it. You may destroy the group by suppressing the active responses of its members to each other and to you. Let them in. And exercise restraint in your use of power. Allow people to criticize you. Don't merely tolerate it, take it in, and be ready to adapt your ways to the ways of the people in the group. Freely concede mistakes. And yet it would be a mistake to take their attacks personally. Often they do not refer to you or your actions. You are there as leader, as boss, as parent, and, if the group includes a few subjects of an ancient regime, as king; you are therefore destined to fall from power. You may be subjected to their rage against oppression, against injustices and injuries they have suffered at the hands of people who have had control over their lives and used it to make them swallow their words, choke back their tears, hold down the free movement of their arms. How wounded they have been!

Only them? Not you? Haven't you ever sat facing another person as if that person were the knife and you were the open wound? Never forget the humiliations, the mean-spirited moments when you lashed out at a friend, the rivalries, the nearly forgotten times when you were not at all masterful, you were the victim—have you already forgotten them? In a group—your nights alone, lost, crying noiselessly into the pillow—will stand you in good stead. Your own war against depression will make you an ally of the anger that people in the group are no longer turning against themselves, but against you.

You will be criticized as much for doing too little as you are for doing too much. How can you keep to the middle way? It is not always possible to judge these things by the immediate reaction of the people around you. Yes, you must be vigilant and take cues from the others—let go of the reins you see them picking up. Yet you must remain your own "locus of evaluation:" the place in yourself where you stand, free and apart from the pressures of others upon you, will be your source of stability now. If you are looking for reassurance from others, you will waver, be forced into hazardous positions, and torn apart.

And you will be vulnerable on both sides. On your right, you will hear people saying that you are too passive, a weakling, you are letting things get out of hand. They will say: if you knew what you were doing you would assume dictatorial powers over the group; you would run a tight ship, stamp out dissent, prevent underground currents from surfacing, control divisive behavior.

On the left, you will hear complaints about your dictatorial powers that are like bites of conscience. They will intensify whatever conflicts you have about assuming a position of leadership. If you are already fearful that leadership has something corrupt about it, your guilt may either cripple you, so that you use your power ineffectively, or numb you, so that you become callous and too removed from the people around you.

Mediation

In this situation, you cannot let yourself be provoked into renouncing your role as mediator. At times you will have to fight a two-front war with the people in the group, refusing the crown that one side wants to offer you, and refusing to abdicate the position that the other side is challenging. If it is wrong to become a policeman, controlling the flow of heavy traffic, it is equally wrong to evaporate after a collision when a firm witness is needed. Be firm too in maintaining that "law and order" is not the law of the group. Resist the temptation in yourself to rely on the more familiar and fascistic modes of order, and oppose it in others.

When things become dangerous, when the group is scapegoating one of its members, when someone looks as if he or she will damage someone else, intercede. A wise leader knows when and how to set limits.

Maybe the only way you can learn this setting of limits—which also involves a tolerance for anger, an ability to keep a calm eye of one's own in the midst of a hurricane—is to practice it among people. Forebear setting limits when your actions would protect someone who does not want or need your protection. And act forcefully when bullying persons are wiping off their boots on another's soul.

Role Definition

In many places the leader has been replaced by a "facilitator." That is such an ungainly word, too specialized. "Catalyst" comes closer to my understanding: that neutral person whose presence is necessary for the elements around to combine and for change to take place. The image I like best is that of a "conductor," someone who knows the score, keeps the measure of things, but is hardly dispassionate. It is the leader's responsibility to make sure each one is heard. Actually, I think it would be better not to derive the metaphor from music, but from physics. Then we might say that the conductor is a person who transmits heat and light, is capable of serving as a channel for the thoughts and feelings of others.

Phase Three

Harmony

Phase Three comes as a time of relief.

Each person knows his or her way around the group; it has become familiar. The free powder of anxiety which, like a light snow, covered everything in the beginning, has melted. Trust runs more easily in all directions.

The person whose leadership the group has challenged has become, for them, another person, no longer a possibly harassing master but an ally, a watchful eye around which the group conducts its affairs. Moments charged with meaning are returned to; a sense of coherence and order becomes palpable as the group, which has been an arena for stories, acquires a repeatable history of its own.

You see, this is a dialectical process. In Phase Three, everything reverses itself: before discord, now harmony; before ambivalence, now a clear purpose. Before, anger against the threat of domination; now, alliance with various sources of strength within the group.

Idealization of Leader

But even here there is a danger. The lure of dependency may temporarily skew the perceptions of the people of the group. They may see you, the leader, as more powerful and good than you are. You may be idealized, courted, have bouquets flung at you. How gratifying this can be! How wonderful everyone feels! What warmth, what love is generated by venerating the leader! *But.* The moral elevation of the leader is at the same time a loss of status for everyone else. And you will have to resist the temptation to become a ministering angel who permits no one a moment of despair and pain.

Dependence/Independence

I've warned you against the danger of dependency. Now I have to turn around and say: only through good experiences of dependency do we get a chance to become caring people. The more serious threat to our well-being comes from the American idea of independence. Independence gets confused with being invulnerable, being utterly self-reliant, needing no one for anything, having enough money to command whatever services one depends on for life. It is simply inhuman, this sort of independence. People feel humiliated when they need help; they try to make themselves so independent of others that the networks of connectedness get snapped off, and people are isolated, not independent.

I do not think it is a bad thing to be dependent for awhile if what you are really after is to be able to walk on your own two feet, and what you need is someone to lean on through a particularly rough part of the way. It is also necessary to know how to allow others to be dependent on you. It is important that you know what you have to give, and how much of it you are willing to give, and that you make this clear.

But the really important thing is that you do not secretly wish to attach the dependent ones to you, that you want them to go their own way, apart from you; that you do not resent their making use of you, and that you feel good will towards their separate existence. When you are conducting a group, you often have to step out of the way to allow people in the group to become interdependent. You often have to underscore the extent to which they are helping themselves and each other so that they do not become focused on getting fed only by you. Now you conduct only when other people stop being conductors.*

Individuation

It occurs to me that the ultimate purpose of groups is to further the process of individuation in each of its members, that the pull towards individuation determines the life course of groups. Small groups function, ideally, as symbolic parents, wise and nurturing and powerful. In relation to them, individuals can manage to give up the phase or way of life they were living and to enter upon a new life. The group can heal its members of the homesickness—the fear and trembling and guilt—brought on by breaking with the past, and simultaneously initiate them into the ardor and bafflements of the present. What the group enables the individual to accomplish is a rite of passage.

*The unabridged essay speaks of a cycle which includes two additional phases: a phase in which a heightened sense of self-definition strains, but does not break, the sense of solidarity; and a phase of endings.

SUGGESTED READINGS

Kaminsky, M. *What's inside you it shines out of you.* New York: Horizon Press, 1974.

Kaminsky, M. *All that our eyes have witnessed, aging, reminiscing, creating.* New York: Horizon Press, 1982.

Koch, K. *I never told anybody: Teaching poetry writing in a nursing home.* New York: Random House, 1977.

Myerhoff, B. *Number our days.* New York: Simon & Schuster, Inc. 1978.

PART V

WRITING: THE WORD UNITES EXPERIENCE: PAST, PRESENT, AND FUTURE

With the written word, poetry or prose, we can conjure up the world of images, feelings, metaphors, stories, and dreams. Past, present, and future coalesce in the word, fact, and fantasy.

Laura Fox describes her voyage as a writer/teacher leading older citizens to get their "tellings onto paper" at nutrition sites and in nursing homes. Her narrative introduces us, insightfully, to the individuals who slowly join her workshops. They submit, with fear and wonder, their early writings as they discover that the words are all there, inside them, waiting to be released.

George Warner, who lived as a gerontocrat, articulates the process of recording family history through the techniques of genealogy. Genealogy fits somewhere between oral history, life review, journal writing, reminiscence, and autobiography. Or, possibly it includes them all. He offers this route as rewarding activity for retired adults, ambulatory or not, as a fulfilling way to connect one's past with the future, a legacy for grandchildren and great-grandchildren.

It is articulation. It is translating something of the self into language which for even the most unlettered human is our uttered being. And if, beyond that, we can engrave the utterances in writing, something of our being remains.

Laura Fox, Founder-Director of TAPROOT WORKSHOPS, Setauket, New York; has been a consultant and teacher of Creative Writing in California and at SUNY, Stony Brook, New York. She works in nursing homes and senior centers. Her writing has appeared in newspapers and journals in Alaska and Israel; she is also a playwright and novelist and the Editor of *Taproot* magazine.

IS IT LITERATURE, IS IT ART?
WRITING WORKSHOPS WITH LITERATE AND ILLITERATE

Laura Fox

My Beginning

My Russian Jewish grandmother, who lived with us, told me stories. She drew for me and peopled a mythic interior landscape, which is still with me. This landscape seems to provide references, recognitions, a sense of the *almost* familiar in my wanderings at home and abroad. Beyond the delightful idioms she gave me. grew a sense of idiom; beyond the faces and gestures she drew, a sense of protoimages. She initiated me into the universal village, the human tribe.

Years later in the early 70s when we were experiencing a bathos of national guilt about the plight of our aged, I thought of her often when I was stricken by the voicelessness of these other grandparents. Where were they; why didn't we hear them? What of the children? When the development vandals had carried the elders off to the retirement villages, the condo tracts, the shopping malls, had their tongues been paralyzed?

At this time I was "at liberty," after an intense 2 year effort to bring "disadvantaged" university students to the writing of English. Before that, I had worked with minority adults in similar programs—trying to bring the inarticulate to voice. What, I thought, of this largest minority of all—the aged. In many ways they were the most disadvantaged in our youth-oriented culture. Shouldn't we be trying to bring them to voice—so our children could hear them, could grow on the stories?

Since I was teaching a writing course in an adult education program at that time, I proposed, to the approval of my director, a course exclusively for older people in which they might stimulate each other to tell stories out of their lives. I would then help them develop techniques for writing these down reasoning that, in this time of the ruptured oral tradition, it was important to find ways of getting tellings onto paper. I foresaw many critical, artistic problems — written folk tales were in themselves an anomaly.

But my first problems were far less esoteric. All the publicity about this original program (in 1973 it was very new, at least in our area) and all the eager inquiries had yielded a first class of two persons. Our older citizens had stayed away in multitudes. I learned the first basic lesson for practitioners in this uncharted field: daytime programs only.

My two eager students, two women in their seventies, and I moved to a local church where we began working one afternoon each week. The two brought two more and quite soon we were twelve, which was for a long time a constant.

It was great fun and easy. My genuine delight in their material and the enthusiasm of their peers seemed to be all that was needed to generate a flood of stories, even poems. I believed that demonstrating that we really cared, really wanted to hear, was all it took to open older people to telling and to inspire them to undertake the struggle of getting tellings onto paper.

I was aware that the people in the group were unrepresentative of the vast majority in our senior citizen population. This was a university community. These people were, in the main, professional retirees still in control of their own lives, with the means to live comfortably and even to seek cultural enrichment.

A Serious Apprenticeship

They had the problems common to all who age in a youth-oriented society, and the real problems of aging in any society. They also had the problems common to well-bred, middle-class people of any age. Here, in this group, which was not a club, they had to make the hard move from conventional attitudes of polite praise to the workshop attitude of "how can this material be made stronger?" They had to be willing to relinquish prettiness of language for honesty and accuracy. They had, in short, to accept all the hard learnings attendant upon a serious apprenticeship in an art. But I had expected this. One has many of these problems in any workshop. And, as in any writing workshop, there were the few who were desperate to publish. For them, the workshop was the vehicle of the last chance. Their desperation threatened to rock the workshop. But weak members grew stronger and the workshop prevailed.

At that time, at least a year before Marc Kaminsky's book describing his poetry groups in senior centers,[1] and years before the book by Kenneth Koch about his poetry workshops in a nursing home,[2] I could lean only on my own previous experiences. I did find in the *Teachers and Writers Collaborative* of New York City a shared teaching philosophy and, although their work was with children, many intriguing ideas in their publications.[3]

When my workshop published a collection of writings[4] reflecting only 6 months of work and resulting in an unsolicited grant, I was convinced of the magic of the method. Essentially it was: (1) enthusiasm about people and their material—even if the work itself was weak; and (2) the strengthening of this work by constructive criticism, e.g., "How can this scene (speech, mood, etc.) be made more vivid (accurate, true, etc.)?" We would never say a work was good or bad, better or worse.

The small grant enabled me to start two new workshops. I decided to go to a large nutrition site in a poor area and to a well-known nursing home. In this first flush of success, armed with my "method," I began at the nutrition site.

At the Nutrition Site

I made several visits to "drum up trade." It was not easy. The staff at the center loved the idea of something "so creative" but they did not help. However, when I finally met with my group, I felt it had been worth the effort. In a dank basement room a large group assembled, few with much interest. They didn't know what to expect. Typical of their acquaintance with writing was the remark of a hearty Irish woman, "I never wrote anything except a laundry list." We laughed. She was not joking.

The Group

The group was fascinating. The largest number were Italian, some from the "old country," some from New York's Little Italy. Others were Irish, Blacks (from the city, from the South, and from the Carribbean); several Germans, Hispanics, two Swedes, two Hungarians, one Jew, and two native Americans—members of a group split off from the Shinnecock Indian tribe of Eastern Long Island. Formal schooling ran from 2 years in a rural Southern schoolhouse to high school in the city.

They introduced themselves to each other and told a bit about their backgrounds. A quarter of them had been orphaned and raised in institutions or foster homes. Most of them were widows. There were two couples, one of which was Shinnecock. Most of the women had worked in factories or as domestic servants. The three men had all been laborers. They ranged in age from middle sixties to middle eighties.

Most were lively and outgoing. We talked about their various backgrounds, their roots (that was before the TV series based on Alex Haley's book), and why that mattered; why stories of the past should be passed on. I told them about my grandmother. One person volunteered a story about her grandfather. We heard about the Irish potato famine in a village in County Cork, about a volcanic eruption in a village in Sicily. They were now as excited as I was. Then I passed out paper. Silence fell. A black woman said bravely, "I can't spell, I didn't have but 2 years schooling in Carolina." Nobody else said anything. I told them that spelling didn't matter at all for this kind of work. We'd just get it down, no matter how, and then we could fix it together. They should write it just as they spoke it and then it would be strong and ring true. There were murmurs of disbelief. I asked the man who had told us so stirringly of his grandfather running away during the potato famine if he'd say the same thing, just the same way, on paper. "Nope," he said implacably, "can't do that."

"Peg said she never wrote nothin' but a laundry list, I never even wrote that much," said another woman. "And anyway, who the hell would care about what I done? I'm nobody."Eileen was articulate and angry.[5]

The Right to Write It

I remembered Tillie Olsen in *Silences* talking about the poor, the marginal, in our society. "How much it takes to become a writer...but beyond that: how much conviction as to the importance of what one has to say, one's right to say it..."[6]

How could I confer on them the conviction of their worth, the importance of what they had to say, their right to say it? I had not met anything like this in my first group. There, with whatever fears or misconceptions, they had come to write. I tried to tell them what I felt about the importance, the uniqueness of each life and why it mattered to tell about it. I talked rather wildly—a passionate mishmash of elementary anthropology, psychology, linguistics.

"Sound like our preacher back home," a black woman said happily. At least they did not disapprove of me but they would not write for me when they really believed they could not. No, it was not quite enough to confer on them the right to say it; they would tell me their stories eagerly, but that wasn't the point. I could not bestow on them the right to write it; they had to believe they could, before they would give themselves the right.

I remembered how the poet Kathleen Kranidas had plunged young children right into the act of poetry.[7] The children had not believed they could make poems. Of course they were not fearful, in the paralyzing way of these older people. Still, I had to do something quickly.

Strategies

I asked them to play a word game with me. Just a game. Faces lightened. They knew word games from TV. The blank white paper was a problem, but I had to use it, since I had no lined worksheets. I asked them to copy the three incomplete sentences I wrote on the board.

1. From the deck of the ocean liner, the people saw...
2. The lost child sat crying in the woods and he saw...
3. The woman was afraid and in her dream she saw...

Several began. Copying was not a great threat. I went around the table helping those who were not writing. "Got my hand crippled-up with arthritis," one
woman said. This was a cover. I could now write for anyone who could not
for any reason. I asked the members who could write easily to help me. Even
so, it took long. Finally, we had the sentences down—with a lot of space after
each one.

Someone grumbled that it felt like school. Someone else asked what happened to the game. "Now—right now, the game," I promised. "Call out to me,
sing right out, the names of birds—any bird." Quickly I erased the sentences
from the board. They all knew some birds. This was easy. Voices competed.
Each one, even the most reticent, contributed a bird. It was fun. The list
grew.

"Now words that tell what birds do?"

'They sing." "They fly." "They make nests."

I wrote "singing," "flying," "nesting," on the board and elicited more till
we had a good list. I asked them to look at the board, then the first sentence,
and to complete it with the name of a bird and the action of that bird. I gave
examples and I assured them that there were no right or wrong answers.
Whatever they chose made it theirs. I realized that several had difficulty
reading the sentences I had written for them. I helped again. We went on to
do the other two sentences.

My hands trembling, I gathered up the papers and read the sentences as
beautifully as I could. I performed them. I wanted them to be impressed.
They were. So was I. They had all, with the exception of one woman who
was on powerful tranquilizers, chosen birds and actions appropriate to the
situation. Many, where there was a choice, had seized a particular mood and
enhanced it. The tones were true. These are a few representative sentences
written that day:

The people on the deck of the ocean liner saw a group of buzzards
feasting on a dead whale.

The people standing on the deck of the ship saw an eagle soaring after
the seagull who was gliding after a sandpiper.

The lost child sat in the woods crying and saw a vulture eating on its
prey; it was very ugly for a child to see.

A lost child sat in the woods and saw a rabbit peeping at her as she was crying and she stopped and lost all fear.

The woman was afraid and in her dream she saw a vulture swooping over her new baby.

The woman was afraid and in her dream she saw a bat flying around and around in her room.

A Teaching Instrument

Now I had a teaching instrument for them, their own work. I told them I would show them how much they already knew about the *artistic* use of language. As I read I pointed out images (I called them pictures) that were particularly strong. I invited them to guess why that was so. They hesitated, not trusting their instinctive responses. Finally Eileen, the angry one, said, "Heck, a vulture could scare the pants off you!" Everyone laughed. "Exactly," I said, "and that's why you chose it." "Well sure," she admitted.

And so it went. I showed them how, with the lost child, some had made frightening pictures, some soothing ones. "But which is right?" someone asked anxiously. I told them that each was right; some had chosen to go with a lost child's fear, others chose to reassure the child. Each had made a choice and then very sensitively created just the right picture to reveal what they had chosen.

"Ain't we something?" Mary said. They all looked pleased. I closed the session by asking permission to keep their papers. And then I bribed them to come the following week by promising to return their work to them beautifully typed. I had decided to call their writing *work* since they were of a generation with respect for work and workmanship. And since they were so pleased with themselves now, I promised that we would play another game, much like this one, next time.

At the next session most of them were there with the addition of several new faces. They were enchanted with their typed work. Typing gave it status. Someone said it looked like print. I agreed as I passed out colored folders for each person's work. As they were inserting their first work into the folders, I passed out worksheets for the new "game."

The Second Step

I told them how much I enjoyed their work. I asked them to do another game with me and they agreed. This exercise[8] was a big leap forward. I prayed that it would seem simple to them, like the last one. I asked them to look at the Xeroxed worksheets which had this on them:

With you
I am a . . .
. . .
Without you
I am a . . .
. . .

They looked puzzled but I thought to myself that they did not seem too afraid. Quickly, lest consternation grow, I asked for names of animals. With some prompting for wilder animals, we got a good, varied list. I need not have worried that this lesson, designed for young children, would seem patronizing. They enjoyed it hugely. I asked for the action words—what animals do—and as before, wrote them on the board below the animals: barking, roaring, leaping.

Then I sat down and asked them to think of someone who is, or was, important to them. "Visualize this person," I suggested. "Try to get a feel of his or her presence." I told them that when they had "gotten hold" of the person, to start writing. I asked them to leave the first line as it was but to complete the second line, which was blank, to tell what that animal was doing.

The form bothered a few, and I told them that it was really like the other thing they did. To my delight, someone asked if they could write more. I told them to go on as the spirit moved them.

Some went to work at once but several looked upset. One woman said she just could not compare a person to an animal. I said that we do it all the time and gave her some examples: strong as an ox, wise as an owl. Someone called out, "A regular snake in the grass!" Everyone laughed. They called out more examples. I had to urge them back to work. As before, I helped several with the writing, although fewer than last time claimed physical disability.

Their work was astonishing. True, strong poems came from many of them. They were enthralled. There was little argument that it was poetry. The lady of the inspirational verse was truly inspired in her poem. She had written:

With you
I am a tiger
stalking through the field
and thicket of your heart.

Some wrote only *With You*. One wrote only *Without You*. Most wrote both. Sally, of the Shinnecock Indian couple, wrote:

With you
I am an elephant

so big and fine
and walkin slow
thinkin elephant things,
such large love.

Without you
I am a mouse
dirty and scared and skinny,
wondering is this
my life. I sit
and wait for you
to do for me.

Her husband Bill wrote:

With you
I am a fox
cunning and smart
as any one around.
In the forest my sharp nose
can smell out all the
different smells
and my sharp ears
can hear the
slightest sound
and my legs can
run me swiftly
into the underbrush.

Without you
this fox
is always on the run
lookin' out for hunters
that stalk me in the woods
to take pot shots at me.
I hide mostly
in underbrush
or the hole in the tree.

Melba, a soft-spoken Jamaican woman who was quite blind, dictated so rapidly I could hardly keep up:

With you
I am a lamb
gentle, bleating
a little lamb that strayed
away on the hillside
bleating. You take me home,
bind up my broken leg.

Without you
I am a barking dog,
a perfect nuisance,
restless, watching for you—
lost, helpless without you.

Eileen, the angry Irish lady who wrote the following lines, remained a difficult but ardent member, until she died 2 years later. She read her poem with irony and bitterness:

With you
I am a pussy cat
against your St. Bernard.

Without you
I am a lost soul
frustrated, but you tell me
I'm very good
for my age.

She wrote, during the 2 years she was with us, almost as compulsively as she talked—jagged, poignant pieces about a mean, impoverished, motherless life in New York's Lower East Side. Although many of our members had rejected her formerly because of her rude, abrasive behavior, they began to accept her as they came to know her through her work. Her death, the first one in that workshop, was a blow to all of us.

Martha, a seemingly jolly lady wrote:

Without you
I am just a little gray mouse
Trying to pretend I am an ape
Swinging and laughing through life.

Ellie, gentle, a recent widow who had never said anything in the group, wrote three moving verses:

With you
I feel content,
Carefree as cows
layin by the shady oak
watchin the world
go by.

Without you
I feel like a traveler
in a strange land
lookin for shelter,
food and water.
I am thirsty,
lost and lonely.

And in a strange country
I am so lost without you
I am a lost glove, just waitin
to be mated up with the other.

Hilda, the dazed lady on strong tranquilizers, wrote the only piece that mixed its metaphors:

Without you
I am a deer, lost, frightened, confused and frustrated
Trying to find a way to get
Back on an even keel.

When I read it, Bill, who had been the fox in the underbrush said, upset, "That don't go—that about an even keel with being a deer."

I asked him why and he mumbled, annoyed with me, something about, "First she's in the woods and then she's on a boat—all mixed up."

Melba, the blind woman, said softly but with irritation, "She admitted she was confused, right in the poem, didn't she? Well, maybe that's why that happened."

We finished on a great high.

Several, on their own, wrote similar poems at home and brought them in to the next session. Without the form or the words on the blackboard, the poems were freer.

Bill wrote:

With you

I can fly the highest
and sing the loudest
than any other bird.

Without you
I turn into a roaring tiger
destroying everything in my path
as I go through the woods
that is in my way.

Sally wrote:

With you
I am as large as
the Blue Ridge Mountains of Virginia
spreading out its beauty
in all directions.

Without you
I am like a sluggish stream of water
looking for a large flow to join
now that spring has come.

"Lessons" and Dreams

After this strong beginning the group moved through many exercises. They demanded "lessons" in the workshop. Soon many were writing at home as well, but only in response to specific assignments. This way of working continued until they were writing so much there was no time for anything else.

They moved through dreams. They wrote their dreams in the first person, present tense. "As if you are in the dream now and it's happening," I urged. Millie, who would become one of our most powerful and prolific writers, wrote:

It's almost morning and I look out of my back window and I see a small blond-haired girl in a long nightgown with a ruffle at the hem and on the long sleeve ends — she is running along my fence as if she is scared. I yell, 'Hey Bill there's a little blond girl running around in the yard, she's about three years old — how the hell did she get in over the fence?' We both run out and when we get there she is on the other side of the fence sitting in a pile of junk and this little boy is just pulling a rusty wire out of the heel of her foot. I rush over and pick up the little girl — she isn't even crying — she just looks up. Now I find myself

walking along Main Street and I am stopping in to the stores and asking does anyone know this child? (I never saw her before). I too am
dressed in a long white nightgown with a ruffle on the hem and at the
sleeve edges. No one seems to know the child. All of a sudden a
woman dashes out of the paper store—never says a word, just grabs
the child from me and starts to walk off and I yell to her, 'You bitch,
you better get her to a doctor before she gets blood poisoning!' and I
wake up.

Others wrote interesting dreams but with somewhat less than Millie's palpable
immediacy. Those who said they did not dream were asked to write
dreamlike memories.

Dreams, and memories as dreams, loosened the prose writing which had
been too self-conscious, and then the group began to write early memories
touched off by specific thematic assignments. At this stage the assignment
gave them a lot of security although, it is interesting to note, they often ignored it and took off on their own. The first of these assignments asked for a
memory of having done something that was naughty or forbidden. This lesson
was enjoyed enormously and some delightful pieces were written. The poem
that touched off the memories was Theodore Roethke's *Child on Top of a
Greenhouse*.[9] It provoked wonderful discussion about the excitement, as well
as the fear, involved in doing the forbidden or the dangerous.

I began every lesson with the reading of one or more poems. This was
not for any critical analysis of the poem. It was to introduce them to new
pleasures in language, to loosen them up, to open a world of possibilities.
They wrote a lot. Some were natural storytellers, others poets. But almost
everyone tried everything. They were enthusiastic and generous with one
another.

The workshop, which continued for 4 years, became the center of their
lives. Mine too. During those years we lost some members to illness, a few to
death. And others came. The basic core group of eight or nine devoted
writers remained constant. Their work appeared in two issues of *Taproot*
Magazine.[10] Some of it was dramatized for a university production which
they attended on opening night. They laughed and wept together.

At a Nursing Home

Almost a year after the beginning of the nutrition site workshop, I began
another at a nursing home. It was a fine private facility of excellent reputation
in a beautiful area. Most of the residents were well-off economically, or had
children who were, but thanks to Medicare and Medicaid there were some
residents from all classes.

Poet-playwright Claire Nicolas White joined me in the work there soon
after I started. We began with about eight residents, acquired more, but often

had far fewer, due to the serious illnesses of many of our members. We were as struck by the vast differences in physical health, from quite hale-looking ambulatory members, to extremely frail or crippled ones, as we were by the wide range in educational and class background. At one end of the spectrum was Mrs. Maynard, an elegant, ambulatory lady, university educated, of wealthy family background. She had always liked to write letters, essays, journals and had begun to write for us shapely, interesting autobiographical stories in a very careful prose. She was impatient with most of the others and was disdainful of our "lessons."

At the other end of the spectrum was Mrs. Bushberry, a merry, frail little lady of ninety-one, wheelchair-bound for many years. She had only a few grades of schooling but had been thoroughly educated, as she used to say, in the school of hard knocks. Hers had been a life of poverty—adventures and misadventures straight out of Dickens—and she saw herself clearly as the *heroine* of the life story she was determined to write. In simple declarative sentences, pure McGuffy Reader, each one starting with I, Mrs. Bushberry wrote a chapter each week, benignly moving through hair-raising episodes. All of us in the workshop, plus a few families and co-workers, waited with bated breath for each new chapter.

Near Mrs. Maynard's end of the spectrum was Mr. Weston, an erect, courtly gentleman of ninety-two, who wrote sonorous ballads in heroic couplets. He told us some salty little tales of the peccadillos of old Long Island characters—baymen and minor bandits—and, after a few months and much flattery from the ladies, he began to write these stories for us.

Somewhere towards the middle was Mrs. Hartly, afflicted since girlhood with crippling arthritis, but eager to translate the brilliantly clear memories of her mining-town childhood into stories. And nearer to Mrs. Bushberry there was Mrs. Dearly, who had been raised in a hotel by ebullient uncles and a staid Quaker grandmother. She had fostered almost 100 children in her lifetime and had almost as many stories to tell. And there were several others. Everyone here was literate and, with the exception of Mrs. Maynard and Mr. Weston, they were as eager to please as good schoolchildren.

I came to the nursing home convinced that the techniques which worked so dramatically at the nutrition site could work anywhere. After all, I had seen the first lessons slash right through all the inequities and the fears and plunge the participants into real writing.

Resistance

Claire, my poet-playwright partner, and I tried. Most seemed confused or vague about what we expected. The alert, intelligent Mrs. Maynard and Mr. Weston balked. She would not, on principle, relate people to animals. He thought it was pointless, kindergarten stuff. At my urging a few people constructed poems mechanically, obviously getting nothing from the process—so different from the other group. I knew that they, although unable to articulate it, had felt the poem happening in them. Their joy, their gut reactions, had made me a believer. So I persisted. But here, although they tried gamely to comply, there was no engagement. Nothing happened for them. When I gave up, miserable, my colleague suggested that we read poems to them.

She read some Whitman; I read some Williams. They relaxed. They liked being entertained. Some listened with seeming pleasure. Some looked glazed. Some slept. I wondered if the glazed or the sleeping heard anything. I wondered later how much any of them could hear. Only after a lively woman impatiently gestured me to wheel her nearer to us did I notice her hearing aid—then two more. "If I turn it up high it buzzes," she explained.

Group Poem

We decided to try a group poem, and explained that each person would contribute one line and we would write it on the board. When I started to erase the animals to make room, Mr. Weston suggested that we not waste it, that we make the poem about animals. Mrs. Maynard agreed to participate "if we didn't get silly." She had nothing against animals. A very quiet woman, who had not yet said anything, said that she liked dogs, that dogs keep us from harm. That became the first line. The quiet woman smiled shyly. This is the poem to which everyone but one, who really slept, contributed—even the glazed people:

> *Dogs keep us from harm*
> *With a dog one is free to roam.*
> *An eagle goes where he pleases,*
> *it represents the United States*
> *where everyone is free.*
> *I used to want to be a butterfly*
> *but not a caterpillar.*
> *We like to watch squirrels and chipmunks*
> *early in the morning,*
> *they always have something to do.*
> *Be industrious like a beaver*
> *if not in body, then in mind.*

They were very pleased when they heard it read. So were we. They had used animals and made metaphor after all. One of the ladies said they ought to do another, so they wouldn't forget how. Someone suggested a Christmas poem, as it was late fall. The talk came round to very special gifts they remembered, not the usual. So that we might get specific details, we gave some examples. This was their second collaborative effort:

A Gift for Christmas

A very sharp knife to peel an apple with.
A comb shaped to fit the head.
A poinsettia plant I couldn't afford.
A little blue box of Battersea enamel
that says "gift of a friend."

The arrival of a longed-for letter.
An evening at the opera.
A big fat check, a winning ticket.

A walk through the meadows with grandchildren.
A good pair of legs, a mended heart.
Accomplishments, things done for others,
Freedoms — of various kinds.
A gift of laughter, the effervescence
of true joy, of inner warmth,
a festival of lights.

This poem, just as it was created that day, was the result of "on-the-hoof" editing. Pleading inability to get everything down fast enough, we let the weakest lines go by, making sure, however, that each person who spoke up had at least one line in the finished piece. The lines of the last verse were created by the two intellectuals. They felt the other lines were lacking in idealistic feeling. Later we would suggest ways of invoking even the noblest feelings through specific images. But for now we let it ride.

Our time was up. Attendants swarmed in to whisk our students off to lunch. Mrs. Maynard brought us a stack of nicely-typed essays. Mr. Weston waited politely until she left, whereupon he handed me several long beautifully-scripted ballads. He said charmingly, "Enjoyed myself more than I expected. But can't call that poetry."

I worried about the glazed ones and the sleepers, but the assistant director assured me that we had gotten remarkable participation. She was truly excited.

Three Distinct Groups

We had a lot to learn here about what to expect of ourselves and them. I was angry with myself for having been so set and so naive.

After a few sessions we knew that it was a very different thing we would be doing here, if we could do it. What would it be if it survived? It did, and became a workshop. Each workshop was proving to be totally different from the preceding one, and this one evolved as three distinct groups.

Mrs. Maynard, by herself, was one group. She continued to write her well-executed stories which my colleague or I critiqued as we would any writer in a university class. Her stories grew more professional, and we and the group enjoyed them whenever there was time. Since our time was limited to 1 hour (our other workshops ran 2 and 3 hours) and the attention span was fragile for so many, we could not allow ourselves this treat very often. But Mrs. Maynard seemed pleased with her special status. To our surprise, after a year or so, she took a flyer into poetry and really enjoyed it. She periodically grew terribly impatient with the "childishness" of the rest of us, but would, after periods of absence or stony silence, return to the workshop.

Mr. Weston, our Edwardian gentleman of the iambic pentameter, Mrs. Bushberry, our *Perils of Pauline* author, Mrs. Hartley and Mrs. Dearly, and several others who came to us later, constituted another unit. They wrote eagerly, were the central group that determined the character of the workshop. "Lessons," which had to be extremely spontaneous, were mainly for them; they required some structure, or at least some point of departure, before they could move into writing. All except Mrs. Bushberry, who moved doggedly from chapter to chapter through her life, one each week, health permitting. This central group loved to do blackboard (collaborative) poems, and became very good at them. Sometimes some of them dictated their own poems, spontaneously, to the scribes.

The third group were those I called the glazed or the sleepers. This group contained one or two real "sleepers," in the movie sense, who would periodically wake up and produce surprising things. Among the glazed were some who were listening, on some level, for they would occasionally make contributions to the group work.

My colleague became the resident teacher there for the next 3 years, with me relieving her when it got too rough emotionally or when she had to be away. So I was able to stay in close touch and learn with her.

Recently, I found a collective poem, produced about a year after this workshop began. The offering of individual lines had grown to the offering of whole verses:

Five Ways of Looking at a Chrysanthemum

1.

Sad looking flower
with prickly white petals
smelling like Chinese food
unforgettable.

2.

Delicate and feathery white
it reminds me of a festive
formal dinner
that made me miss
a Saturday afternoon
football game.
The flower looks at me
through a yellow core
like a watching, patient eye
viewing life as it rushes by.

3.

The white flower
like a firework
bursting in the air
smells sweet
like the perfume Chanel
which my sister gave me.
It feels like rubber.

4.

The small one, reddish pink
strange smelling,
sweet but earthy.
The large one
a dark center
a sweet odor
feathery, graceful
and starlike.

5.

I always think of chrysanthemums
on Election Day
because I saw so many people
wearing them at the polls
in New York City.
The clean smell is soothing.
I will hang it in my closet
so when the door opens
Chrysanthemums!

I had never, before our experience in the nursing home, favored using group poetry beyond the initial session in any workshop. I had admitted that the group poem was a good device for loosening people up, helping them to deliver lines less self-consciously, since they were not responsible for the total effect. It helped to establish camaraderie in a new group. But I felt that the group poem was just another word game.

I felt, too, that many of the leaders of the rapidly proliferating poetry workshops were using the group poem as an end in itself—an easy out, producing what looked like poetry. They got a product they could show, that gave some momentary pleasure to the participants while obviating the real process, which had to be solitary, inside one individual, but which yielded poetry.

I think now that while I was not wrong, I was narrow. I had failed to see the collaborative poem as a teaching instrument. With vocal "on-the-hoof" editing by the group leader, it can be an effective teaching technique in work with the very old and the very ill. Our members in the nursing home taught me that it was of critical importance for people to speak out, reach out, touch each other, even if minimally. Here, the fight against the encroaching isolation of the person was the primary struggle. Before people could tell stories or make poems they had to be aware, even a little. Without some sense of the self, of others, the environment, what would one say—to whom? Being in life had to come first.

So we brought flowers, stones, shells, lockets, pictures, parsley, into the workshop. People handled and smelled and passed things to one another, even the sleepy ones. We brought things of bright color, of pungency, of rough texture and smooth—water and sand and seeds. And then sometimes the group would make a poem, starting perhaps with something just held. I learned that it really didn't matter what they started with.

Claire Nicolas White, in writing of these collaborative poems for the third collection of workshop writings[11] said, ". . . the result is, on some days, a stronger and more honest expression of the feelings than the individual writing efforts."

No One Way

So in this kind of workshop—the third—new ways again had to be found. Clearly there was no one way, no *method*. There were techniques, some useful here, some there. In time, as the workshops grew in number, my teaching colleagues and I collected a "big bag of tricks."

During the next few years we became an organization with a staff of four teachers. I began new workshops with new colleagues who would then take over while I went to other places. We worked in other nutrition centers, other nursing homes, and in community groups like the first group, which has continued unbroken and is thriving today. And we went into schools as well, so children could meet grandparents and hear their stories. To be sure, this was not the same as having a resident grandmother telling tales on the long winter evenings, but the children responded joyously. The need is there; the voices to fill this need are also there—somewhere.

As the workshops developed, so did my conviction that anyone who can feel, think, speak—can write. And all over the country poets, teachers, and just plain people with golden ears, are proving this.

"But what are you getting?" many have asked, "Is it literature, is it art?"

It is articulation. It is translating something of the self into language, which for even the most unlettered human is our uttered being. And if, beyond that, we can engrave the utterances in writing, something of our being remains.

Walt Whitman, speaking of a vanished Indian tribe, says in *Yonnondio*:[12]

No picture, poem, statement passing them
  to the future
Unlimn'd they disappear.

A workshop member who was losing her sight said, "I want people to see me, to know I was here." And another one, harking back to her Southern Baptist childhood, said, "We are raising up our voices, they going to hear us. Glory be, we are bearing witness!"

Definition

What we do is close to poetry therapy, for the act of writing honest poetry brings revelation, liberation, transcendence. We focus on the work; I do not mean the *works*, although these are valuable and often beautiful. I mean the *working*, because that is a powerful force for growth at any age. Such work requires life review, but with the psyche, led by the need for artistic choices, selecting what it wants, what it can deal with. Indeed, our work is close kin to the work of oral historians, but it requires of the writer-respondent a different kind of commitment—to ongoing work.

I think I work to evoke this commitment to one's own development because I must keep proving to myself that at the center we stay green, capable of new growth, to the end of our days. I do this for myself.

I think too, that I work so that at least in the microcosm of the workshop none shall go unlimn'd. Probably, I do this for my grandmother.

NOTES

[1]Kaminsky, M. *What's inside you it shines out of you.* New York: Horizon Press, 1974.

[2]Koch, K. *I never told anybody.* New York: Random House, 1977.

[3]Teachers and Writers Collaborative and Teachers and Writers Magazine, 84 Fifth Avenue, New York City 10011.

[4]*Taproot*, a journal of senior citizen writing, winter 1974-1975 Taproot Workshops, Inc., Box 2-567, Setauket, New York, 11733.

[5]The teaching situations described throughout are factual; the names of participants in workshops are not.

[6]Olsen, T. *Silences.* New York: Delacorte Press, 1978, p. 27.

[7]From an unpublished work by poet, fiction writer, Kathleen Kranidas — techniques shared with many colleagues by this generous and brilliant teacher.

[8]ibid.

[9]Roethke,T. *Collected Poems* New York: Doubleday, 1966, p. 43.

[10]*Taproot*, spring/summer 1977 and *Taproot*, winter 1978-1979, Taproot Workshops, Inc., Box 2-567, Setauket, New York, 11733.

[11]White, C.N. *Taproot* No. 3. Taproot Workshops, Inc., Box 2-567, Setauket, New York, 11733.

[12]Whitman, W. *Collected poems of Walt Whitman, E.* Holloway Ed., Garden City, New York: Book Club Associates, 1926, pp. 432-433.

Pen and typewriter - requisites for Mr. Warner at work.

It (genealogy) is a creative experience requiring imagination, exploration, risk and boundless curiosity . . . [that] provides some meaning to existence.

George A. Warner, Certified American Lineage Specialist; 1902-1982, was the former mayor of Greenbelt, Maryland, a government "planned community" under President Franklin D. Roosevelt. He had been a Senior Accountant, and the Executive Director of the Mayor's Committee on Problems of the Aging in Hagerstown, Maryland. Author of *Greenbelt, the Cooperative Community* , Mr. Warner instructed, assisted, and counseled other gerontocrats in genealogy – both by mail across the country and abroad any by direct encounters in Hagerstown and Washington, D.C., working with 75 older persons at a time.

"RENEWMENT . . . NOT RETIREMENT"
GENEALOGY, THE RECORDS OF OUR LIVES

George Warner

Over the years I have been saddened to hear many of my contemporaries complain that they have no point at which to begin their family history. Or, that there is no history, because their families emigrated to the United States during this century from many parts of the globe and there is no one left in their native towns to tell of the beginnings.

Yet they yearn to review their lives and provide some meaning to their existence. They tell bits and pieces to grandchildren and are often considered senile because they may repeat certain stories to illustrate their past importance. But when asked for specific continuity to their lives, these same folks may grow silent.

To many of them I advise that the place to start is in your own home with what you already know, what you have experienced in bringing up your own families. If you find gaps in your memory, I continue, fill them in from sources like town census reports, relatives' tales, photographs, letters, date books, and calendars. Above all, I urge, get a tape recorder and start talking into it. Let a son or daughter, a grandchild or great-grandchild provide questions. One memory often stirs another, and another.

Most important, it is the little memories that count. More than the major events of one's life, the joy is in remembering a first ride in an auto, a child's birth, talking over one's first telephone, a severe snowstorm when the electricity went off—if one had electricity—or one's arrival in this country, with all the hopes and fears connected with it.

Today's older adults bridge a time of history which has produced incredible changes in life-styles due to the introduction of technology. We have so much to share with the youth of today to help them make connections with their lives. It may sound too strongly put, but I feel that we have a responsibility to share the details and values of our lives with our children and their children, and theirs.

Now let me begin with the major step many of us are forced to take from active participation in the work force to "retirement," a time which can challenge us to reflect, and then make new beginnings, or withdraw into feelings of inadequacy and powerlessness.

Retirement, a New Way of Life

The American College Dictionary's definition of retirement includes, among other things, the act of retiring; removal from service, office, or business, and withdrawal into privacy or seclusion. Statistics reveal that this is a prescription for early death.

Peter A. Dickinson, in his book *The Complete Retirement Planning Book*, takes issue with that definition which he says "smacks of retreat, withdrawal, seclusion, removal from circulation, elastic stockings, and Windsor rockers."[1] He feels that it is a time to enjoy different life-styles, follow second careers, dream and follow new dreams. He calls it "renewment" rather than "retirement," a viewpoint with which I heartily concur.

Retirement is, to a large extent, a new way of life, even though, for the best satisfactions, it should be built upon what one has learned during his or her so-called productive years. Retirement means freedom from dictation by others, regulated work schedules, worry about getting ahead, and saying what is expected to impress those who have the power to mold our thoughts, control our verbal expressions, set deadlines, and tell us where and how to live. Of course, this is predicated upon the possession of enough financial security to be able to make a few choices about the way we live. It is also determined by the degree of good health we are privileged to sustain. But, within these limits, we are freer to choose what we wish to do with our remaining years and whether we wish them to be contemplative or active in contributing to ourselves, our family, and our community.

A happy alternative to stagnation, among many others, is genealogical research or building a family history. And, if one chooses this occupation, it is useful to start planning prior to the day when one receives the "pink slip."

The word "genealogy" is derived from two Greek words, *genea*, or descent, and *logos* meaning discourse. It is classed as a social science, and as stated by Ethel W. Williams, Ph.D., in her book *Know Your Ancestors*, it "contributes to and coordinates with many cognate fields of learning, such as history, biography, geography, sociology, law, medicine and linguistics, to name but a few." [2]

She notes, "family history as it contributes to the history of the local community, the country, the state, and the nation, is the basis for all history." In my searches into family history, both for myself and others, I have been greatly enriched. These searches have brought home to me much of history and geography which I was prone to neglect as a student. I find it is also a creative experience requiring imagination, exploration, risk-taking, and boundless curiosity. If the genealogical bug once bites you, you are doomed. Never again will you be completely happy except when attempting to trace the elusive ancestor, whether yours or that of another; or retracing your own school years through elusive records in dusty files elsewhere in the world than where you now live.

Where to Begin

Start in your own home with your own family. That is where one finds the first evidences of family history. Talk to as many immediate relatives as you can to "pick their brains" and memories while they are still around and available to pass on family information. The older living relatives should be contacted as soon as possible for they have better knowledge of the family's earlier history. Long-time friends of the family are another excellent source. [3]

An article in the Parade Section of The Washington Post, entitled *Up the Family Tree* by Jeane Westin, carried a photograph which accents my point. It was a picture of the Steele family, taken at a family reunion. It showed six generations, from a great-great-great-grandmother, age one hundred, to her great-great-great-granddaughter, age ten months. Under the picture was the statement "There should be no trouble tracing this family tree." Very true, but if not already accomplished, the one-hundred year-old great-great-great-grandmother should be interviewed without delay. Much of my own family history was supplied by an upstate New York genealogist at the age of ninety-eight.

If you are able to interview family members personally, take along a notebook and pencil or a tape recorder. Record what they tell you, and if they are not completely certain of some of the facts, record that also. If the relatives or family friends live at a distance, type out a questionnaire that they can easily fill in, sign, and return in a stamped, self-addressed envelope which you will provide with your letter of inquiry.

Set up your family history, starting with yourself, the person about whom you know the most. Start with your name, birth date, and birthplace, marriage date and place, and to whom married. Include the names of your father and the maiden name of your mother. Enter your wife's date and place of birth, and the name of her father; the maiden name of her mother should be recorded also. Where deaths have occurred, the date and place of death should be noted as well as the place of burial. This completes your generation. Then you tackle your parents' generation. Continue to work back, generation by generation if it is at all possible.

Write everything down, noting the sources of your information. To possess a set of facts which cannot be proven is frustrating. All entries, to the extent possible, should be substantiated by documentation. Whatever cannot be substantiated should be so indicated together with a notation as to the unverified source.

Other Family Records

In your home or the homes of relatives, particularly of parents and grandparents, you may find much of value for your family history. There you may find some original records which can be considered as evidence to support your statements. They may include deeds to land, birth certificates, marriage certificates, death notices, wills or estate settlements, funeral records, school diplomas, social security records, employment records, lodge records, letters, diaries, memory books, photograph albums and newspaper clippings. A letter I found which had been written to my great-grandfather by a family member in another state, addressing him as "Dear cousin" enabled me to connect him with an earlier generation.

Old family photographs are often useful. You should look on the reverse side of each picture to see if it identifies the person or persons and gives a date and/or place or refers to an occasion. One of my greatest frustrations has been that I discovered many photographs, purported to be family pictures, which cannot be identified because no one took the trouble to write on the reverse side. If you find pamphlets containing church histories, they can be helpful. Often they list family members with the dates when they were christened, married, or became members of the church. Visits to graveyards containing the remains of family members will often provide information, giving dates of birth and death and, sometimes, relationships and occupations either carved on the gravestones or available in the cemetery office.

Family traditions, handed down through successive generations, are usually oral. They are often embellished and distorted in the telling but they may, also, provide elements of truth. Such traditions, unsupported by documentary evidence, are good only if within the personal knowledge of the person making the statement. In such cases, one should write down the story as told and record the name and address of the person by whom it was told. It can be utilized in a family history to provide color, but it can be accepted only with reservation and that should be clearly stated.

Other Research

Having gathered as much information as you can from family records and talks with relatives and family friends, the next best place to visit would of course be the localities where your ancestors lived. There you could conduct a firsthand search of the homes, public buildings, and town and city and county records. Too often, however, because of the distance from home and consequent expense, the best place to repair to is the nearest library which has records devoted to genealogy and family history.

Carefully select your library. Some have excellent records. Get acquainted with the librarian in charge and state your particular interests. Find out how they catalogue their books and what special collections they have which might be useful to you.

When working with books or pamphlets, your work sheet should record the title, author's name, publisher's name, and place and date of publication, all of which should appear on the title page of the publication. For manuscript material, enter the author's name, the title as catalogued by the library, and the page number or numbers from which the data has been extracted.

Here is a summary of these procedures:

The offices of the Town or City Clerk usually contain family records such as those relating to births, marriages, divorces, and deaths.

County records cover land grants, deeds, wills, estate settlements, appointments of estate administrators, appointments of guardians, marriage licenses and, sometimes, copies of marriage certificates.

State archives include state census records, vital records, and many early state records. Among the records useful in family research are early marriage licenses, land grants, military muster and payrolls, pension records, immigration and naturalization records, tax lists, and the like.

Federal records, usually found in the National Archives or the Library of Congress, each located in Washington, D.C., comprise census records, land records (patents and bounty land papers), military records (service records, pension applications and death records of pensioners), shipping and passenger lists, immigration records and passport applications. They also include records of the U.S. District Court, Circuit Court of Appeals, and the U.S. Supreme Court.

The National Archives in Washington provides so many tools for use by the genealogist or family searcher.[3, 4]

What Genealogy Has Meant to Me

Having searched records relating to my paternal and maternal ancestors over a number of years, I envisioned an interesting means of helping others with similar interests. Therefore, I decided to make application for certification as either a Genealogist, an American Lineage Specialist, or a Genealogical Record Searcher. I was accepted as an American Lineage Specialist, with the result that I have received requests from practically every state in the Union. I have been engaged in interesting work and have made a host of friends. I feel that my work has contributed towards the preservation of family units through stimulating interest and pride in their past family connections. At the present time, at least, it can be done before many families are broken up by divorce or some of their members decide to live together without benefit of clergy. I hope that many families can be held together before the work of the genealogist becomes more difficult if not impossible.

This is only a partial exposition of the subject. I feel that genealogical research can become an excellent occupation for the retiree. It can provide a source of additional income with which to supplement an already meager pension or social security payment, each of which is, at present, seriously threatened. It is a way to enjoy the excitement of detective work without producing victims. It permits one to relearn history and geography. It permits one to relive the lives and experiences of his or her forebears, and to reflect on one's own existence. Above all, in the words of my late second cousin, Rose Geraldine (D'Allesio) Ryan, it "provides continuity for our own lives."

NOTES

[1]Dickinson, P.A. *The complete retirement planning book: Your guide to happiness, health and financial security*, New York: Elsevier-Dutton Publishing Co., Inc., 1976.

[2]Williams, E.W. *Know your ancestors: A guide to genealogical research*, Rutlandt, Vermont: C.E. Tuttle Co., Inc., 1960.

[3]Colket, M.B., & Bridgers, F.E. *A guide to genealogical records*, Washington, D.C.: U.S. Government Printing Office, Superintendent of Documents, Washington, D.C. 20402.

[4]*Federal population census pamphlet*, Washington, D.C.: National Archives Trust Fund.

PART VI

ART EXPERIENCES ACCESSIBLE TO ALL

The visual arts offer a range of materials through which older persons, experienced or inexperienced, can express their subjective visions. With guidance, they manipulate the clay, wood, paint, wire, paper, string – shaping, expressing, and communicating their personal statements. Although the visual arts are generally considered to be nonverbal, the following practitioners, as you will note, often use the silent arts as stimuli for the written and spoken word.

Georgiana Jungels is an art therapist whose clinical experiences enable her to assess the needs of her clients and prescribe programs for them. She presents us with methods for adapting media to the concerns of the individual. The symbiotic relationship of verbal and nonverbal language for improved group communication is evident in her work.

Pearl Greenberg, as an educator and gerontologist, speaks of the increasing number of well, idle, disabled, and isolated elderly who can be served through the visual arts. She points out the urgency for special training for arts educators who have never worked with the elderly, additional arts training for those who have been working with the elderly for years, and new college programs in the arts and gerontology.

Gail Porter introduces us to a workshop series in photography. Photography, only recently acknowledged as a viable art and skill for senior programs, requires focus, perception, and imagination. This author recognizes the resistance and apprehension which melt away as the new challenge promises a sense of accomplishment.

197

*. . . I try to use basic human language rather than
'art language' . . . words like 'draw' often prompt
people to respond, 'I can't' . . . Instead . . . I might
say, 'Move the pencil the way you like to move your
hand.'*

Georgiana Jungels, Registered Art Therapist; is Director of Art Therapy Studies at the State University College, Buffalo, New York. She is Administrative Program Coordinator for the Buffalo Psychiatric Center; President of the American Art Therapy Association; author, filmmaker, therapist, and artist.

"LOOKS LIKE THE STARTING OF A HOUSE"
ART THERAPY AND THE OLDER ADULT[1]

Georgiana Jungels, ATR

Between the moment in which a person whispers a single word about an art expression and the time in which members of the group openly share their comments and responses, there occur many progressive experiences upon which client and therapist can build communication.

I always learn so much from the older people I meet through shared art experiences. I have worked with older adults in different settings: community centers, senior centers, colleges, hospitals, and nursing homes. I have had varying job titles and roles: art specialist, artist, art educator, art therapist. The common element is *art*. Art-as-art, art-as-activity, art-as-vocation, art-as-education, art-as-therapy.

Art as Therapy

In the following paragraphs, I would like to share some of these experiences with you. They illustrate to some extent what I have learned from the older people in my geriatric art therapy groups, and give an overview of some of the structures I have found helpful in encouraging and fostering increased communication skills among institutionalized older people.

Many of them begin in art therapy with limited communication skills. Some are almost nonverbal because of physical handicaps, retardation, ap-

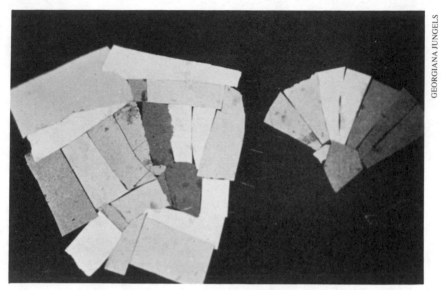

GEORGIANA JUNGELS

1   An array of colors and a fan.

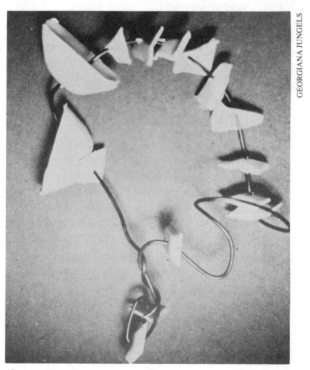

GEORGIANA JUNGELS

2   A scenic railway with seats to sit on.

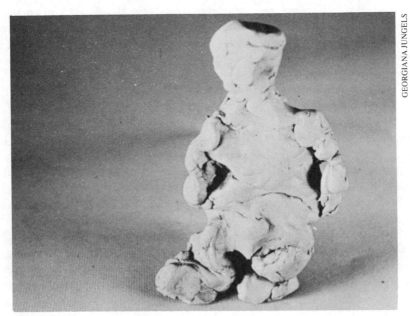

GEORGIANA JUNGELS

3   A man thinking about his neighbor.

prehension, and/or long-term institutionalization. Often their visual communication skills are as limited as their verbal skills.

How to Begin

Initially I search for ways in which the older person can begin to express thoughts and feelings. I offer each one as many choices as possible to stimulate their interest; for example, one may select a particular color, some paint, or a piece of paper, wood, wire. The color might suggest subject matter; paint can be touched to a paper to make "dots" or moved with a sponge for "just colors;" a piece of paper can be torn into "raindrops" or cut and arranged into "an array of colors and a fan" (Figure 1); wood pieces can be arranged into "a village" or "a chip pile on a farm in the state of Virginia;" wire can be twisted and turned into a "circle" or "a scenic railway with seats to sit on" (Figure 2). After selecting a particular size/shape/color/feel/smell/of a piece of clay, a person may squeeze and pinch a "rock," or roll and balance a "tower," or roll and assemble a clay coil "bell," or make "a man thinking about his neighbor" (Figure 3).

Basic Language

During these beginning experiences, I try to use basic human language rather than "art language." I have found that words like "draw" often prompt people to respond "I can't" . . . "I don't know how" . . . "I never could do that."

Perhaps this is because the older person may have developed certain standards for a "drawing" and therefore may feel that he or she cannot meet them. Instead of asking a person to draw, I might say, "move the pencil . . . move it however it feels comfortable . . . move the pencil the way you like to move your hand."

Different Responses

Each of these beginnings in art therapy communicate to the therapist information about the maker. People work at different paces because of preference, attention span, physical abilities, and environmental circumstances such as medication, scheduling, and mealtimes. Some people use many media; others use only one. Some express variety within one media; others repeat shapes and subject matter frequently enough so that interpretation might range from symbolic content, to organic brain damage.

Some people can work in media which involve multistep skills, e.g., painting with cake watercolors which requires taking a brush, dipping the brush in water, rubbing the wet brush on the chosen color, and applying the wet paint brush to the paper; other people can work only in media which involve one-step skills, e.g., painting with a brush which has previously been immersed in liquid nontoxic paint and requires only that the painter lift the paint-filled brush and place it on the paper.

Building Personal Strengths

In working with needy older persons I have found it necessary to analyze each art medium according to: skills required, safety, and developmental stages of complexity. There are hundreds of ways of painting, modeling, printing, drawing, assembling. Each older person has personal strengths to build upon. But often these strengths can be discovered only by very close observation. When an older person seemingly cannot work in an art process, it may be because the particular medium offered for the art process requires complex sequencing, or produces glaring reflections, or irritates the skin and lungs, or exposes the person's weaknesses rather than strengths.

Adult Language

Often, a media analysis suggests using basic art materials such as tempera paint, chalks, wood pieces, crayons, and clay. Inasmuch as these materials are often considered in our culture as "kindergarten" materials, I have found it important to use accepted "adult language" such as "wood sculpture" instead of "wooden blocks." Crayons in the No. 8 Crayola box are immediately associated with kindergarten by my clients; but crayons in a long, flat, compartmental artist's box are not. Reproductions, slides, and books of contemporary sculpture also offer acceptablility to the basic shape wood sculptures that an older adult may make with available wood pieces.

Offering Stimuli

Because many of the older people with whom I work are not living in rich sensory environments, it is important to offer stimuli—a group happening—in the art therapy sessions. These shared experiences seem to help each person's responses to "awaken" and are often followed by increased participation and communication. Ideally, stimuli offer opportunities to respond from many different personal sources: memory, reality, imagination, association. Sometimes this stimulus is a book, a film, slides, movements, exhibits, or the art materials. Usually group or individual needs, questions and discussion, or the qualities of a particular art medium suggest appropriate stimuli.

For example, an 18-inch piece of plastic-coated wire can be identified and discussed on many levels: physical qualities, uses, associations. In each person's hands this 18-inch piece of plastic-coated wire may be turned and connected to be "a mirror," "a perfect circle," "a wreath;" or made into a pair of "glasses" by a partially sighted woman who months before broke her glasses in an outburst of anger at a staff member and now expresses the desire to have a new pair; or described by an often-angry woman as "telephone wire—you can call someone you love;" or described by a man with total blindness "it feels like a tidal wave;" or made into an untitled piece which later during group discussion is described as:

"looks like a pig being held by its tail"

"looks like a donkey"

"the little ones look like the caps of the waves

of the ocean; you see them when you stand by the

shore"

"looks like an Indian"

"looks like John with his headgear"

Each of these descriptions is a personal contribution to the group interaction and shared individual thought processes, language skills, and image association. The last example leads into a more detailed discussion of art therapy experiences which seem to heighten communication within the group.

The most basic principle, perhaps already obvious, is a group environment based on acceptance and encouragement of each individual's expression of feelings, interests, memories, concerns, and abilities. Each older person's progression is unique. At the same time there are often similar experiences, though not necessarily sequential, which are part of this process toward increased communication.

"I'll Just Watch"

Many times an older person will participate initially in a group by watching what other people are doing until he or she sees what is happening and feels comfortable with the therapist, the group members, and the activity. One seventy-five year-old woman watched intently as some of the people in the group were doing crayon rubbings of room surfaces and/or arranged paper pieces. Whenever I had previously invited her to participate in an art activity, she would smile and say in very slow broken English, "Oh, I'm too old; I'll just watch." Noticing her interest in the rubbings, I brought her some string and asked her to take it and drop it on the table in front of her. After she did, I placed a piece of paper over the string and demonstrated how to rub the crayon. She began to slowly rub across the paper. I then explained that the crayon, paper, and string were for her to use as much as she wanted and I would be back in a few minutes. When I returned, she had written what appeared to be many names diagonally across the left side of the paper. I asked her about the names and she said they were "messages." I asked her to whom the messages would go. She said, "To Emma." I said, "Why, that's you! Why are you sending messages to yourself?" She replied, "To be remembered." After a moment, I told her I would remember her wavy silver hair, her soft speaking voice, her dark eyes, and her smile. She smiled and squeezed my hand.

Common Art Materials

In the personal expression of each older person's use of the same art materials there are unlimited variations. If there is acceptance of different ways of doing things with one art material, an older person may be less hesitant to share his or her own particular style and subject matter. Several rolls of wallpaper may prompt conversations about the interiors of homes, techniques for hanging wallpaper, and the appropriateness of each pattern for particular rooms. The art work following such a discussion was derived from each person's prior experiences. This in turn stimulated further verbalization:

This house is in the coal mining region in Scranton, Pa. We had lace curtains at the windows, straight down. When we washed them, we washed them in Lux and put them on stretchers.

Those look like chimneys. Our curtains were yellow and white. Flowers, I think. We lived in New York. Some houses were white and pink. I never noticed where the door handle is—it was always open.

Or a box of small varied wooden pieces may be arranged and described differently by each person. For example:

Looks like the starting of a house.

Born and raised in Shenandoah, Pa.
Population 7500
Our backyard was the coal mine
And we lived by the railroad
It was a coal mining town
with six mines quite a few homes
quite a few people
The woman kept house
and went out to pick coal
and the men went to the mines
the people played cards and
had all kinds of games.

These shared variations of expression can lead to group discussions of common feelings, varied life-styles, and multiple ways of responding to crisis situations.

Sharing is important, for it increases the older person's communication skills. Many older people begin to share their art expression first with the therapist and then through the therapist, gradually may extend this sharing to include other group members.

Because this provides the impetus for increased communication, I offer participants the ongoing opportunity to exhibit their work in the art therapy room. If the art work is also accompanied by typed descriptions written or dictated by the maker, the exhibits provide both visual/tactile and verbal stimulation for conversation. It appears to be easier to look at a picture, touch a sculpture, and read a description than it is to go up to another person and initiate a conversation. I've noticed that people who rarely get up out of their chairs will spontaneously walk over to see an exhibit area; people who never ask questions in the group or rarely respond verbally to the comments of other group members will stand and carefully read descriptions accompanying exhibited art work.

One seventy-eight year-old woman with a severe speech impediment initially resisted participation in the art therapy discussions. After she had completed a sequence of four drawings, she wrote descriptions of them which she read to us. In this context we were able to train our ears to understand her. Here are her statements.

Milkweed

Buttercups and trees

A Creek. The log cabin was up above the creek.

Wild flowers blooming among the wild hay near roadway which in Colorado went up into the hills. We went up and got a wagonload of poles to make a cowshed.

These written descriptions are like small stories.

Shadow Show

Occasionally a group story develops out of the art work of each group member. For example, cut-out paper images of a fence, bird, mammoth, small dog, mountains, and moon can be elaborated and related by the group into a shadow show with a story like: "When the moon came up over the Colorado Mountains, a small dog and a mammothlike animal watched a bird fly over the fence." I have noticed an increase in group conversation about each person's art work whenever work was shared via a shadow show or slides.* Perhaps this is because shadow and slide shows offer older persons in a group — especially the older person with limited eyesight — the opportunity to see intensified colors and enlarged shapes and to share experiences.

The Exhibit

As group members increase their communication skills it becomes essential to provide a link to people outside the group. One way to do this is to invite the people in the group to participate in an exhibit beyond the walls of the geriatric art therapy rooms. Even the preparations for an exhibit offer many therapeutic possibilities. There are many choices to be made: which art work to display; whether or not to be identified in this more "public" exhibit; the possibility of "selective" framing in which a person shows only what he or she likes about a particular picture. Just trimming and mounting a picture makes it special and may raise a person's estimation of the value of the work. As one woman said when she handed me a drawing "This is to put on the wall."

Cultural Considerations

Cultural and historical backgrounds are revealed in our work in many ways. I first began to be aware of this when one of my female geriatric clients expressed surprise at the fact that I was married and had three children and still worked. She told me that her husband "made her quit her job as a nurse" as soon as they were married, in the 1920s. There are significantly different

---

*Cut-paper images can be used to make a shadow show by simply holding the paper pieces up to a rear-projection screen or stretched sheet with a light source behind the paper piece.

individual and cultural attitudes toward women combining marriage, children, and employment today; and as a result, I have taken a closer look at some of these different attitudes in my geriatric clients and in myself.

For example, how can a young female art therapist living in the center of a large urban community adequately communicate with clients who are over sixty-five years of age and reside in a rural institutional community? I must know about historical events, familial structures, sexual roles, religious beliefs, occupations, labor patterns, trends in mental health treatment, and the activities, objects, events, living styles, and peoples of the past 100 years. How else can I communicate with a person about blackouts, food rationing, flexaphones, eisenglas, Lux, magic lanterns, grits, farina, and God in the electricity? My resources are books, newspapers, films, stories, interviews, antique shops, garage sales, grandparents, aunts and uncles, and each older person with whom I work.

As an art therapist in geriatrics, I need to know about the turn-of-the-century, the twenties, the thirties, the forties, the fifties in terms of events, roles, history, and styles, but I also need to learn about current experiments, observations, clinical studies, and models of human memory.

Art therapists need to examine the very subtle nuances of their interactions with geriatric clients. I would also suggest that we look at cultural influences on the field of art therapy itself. How is the history of art therapy and the current "body of knowledge" affected by recent work in perception? What information in the future will suggest that we re-examine our present attitudes?

NOTES

[1]Sections of this material are reprinted from *To Be Remembered, Art and the Older Adult in Therapeutic Settings* (Jungels) with permission from the publisher, Potentials Development, Inc. 775 Main Street, Suite 325, Buffalo, New York 14230.

SUGGESTED READINGS

American Art Therapy, Inc. *American Journal of Art Therapy*. American Art Therapy Association, Two Skyline Place, Suite 400, 5203 Leesburg Pike, Falls Church, VA 22041.

Jungels, G. *To be remembered, art and the older adult in therapeutic settings*. Buffalo, New York: Potentials Development, Inc., 1982.

Schonewolf, H. *Play with light and shadow, the art and techniques of shadow theater*. New York: Reinhold Book Corp., 1968.

Terkel, S. *Working*. New York: Pantheon Books, 1972, 1974.

Zwerling, I. The creative arts therapies as real therapies. *Hospital and Community Psychiatry*, (Vol. 30) Dec. 1979, No. 12, 841-847.

Hands like to weave at the Runnels Rehabilitation Center, New Jersey.

The well elderly are not passive learners; they need to and want to share in the planning, organizing, and implementing as well as the evaluation of their programs.

Pearl Greenberg, M.A., Ed.D. Fine Arts; is a Professor in the Department of Fine Arts at Kean College, New Jersey. As a gerontologist, she leads a course entilted *Art Media in Gerontology*. She is the co-editor of *Lifelong Learning in the Visual Arts* and author of numerous books and articles. Dr. Greenberg is Vice-President of the National Art Education Association; a founding member and past President of the University Council for Art Education. She is Chairperson of the Higher Education Division, Art Educators of New Jersey; she trains, places, and supervises college students leading art programs in nursing homes, hospitals, and senior centers within the state.

APPROACHES TO TRAINING AND CURRICULUM DESIGN IN THE VISUAL ARTS FOR THE ELDERLY

Pearl Greenberg

Every community has older adults looking for places where they can go to meet others, socialize, and learn something new or enhance knowledge already gained earlier in their lives.[1] Increasingly, these elderly want to learn to use time rather than just fill it. Those who are exploring the visual arts want skills and opportunities to express themselves, not simply for leisure but for aesthetic experiences which can be part of their lives.

While we cannot assume that every older person with whom we come in contact is going to be interested in the arts, there are many who may not even be aware—who have never before had free time to find out—that they have some latent talents in the visual arts. Unless given the opportunity to try out quality training, they will never realize their potential. Of course, among the geriatric population which numbers over 24 million at this writing, there must be as large a proportion of experienced painters, sculptors, weavers, potters, and printmakers as in any other group of adults![2] They are usually the self-actualizers who go on creating as long as their vigor allows.

College Programs

More and more, people in the later phases of life are choosing to attend college and adult education programs in the visual arts. Many colleges allow them to sign up to fill vacant seats in courses, often free of charge or at a minimal cost for registration.[3] Thus no special program is planned; they join the regular students as members of the class. Some enjoy this keenly and become class members with ease following the regular curriculum.

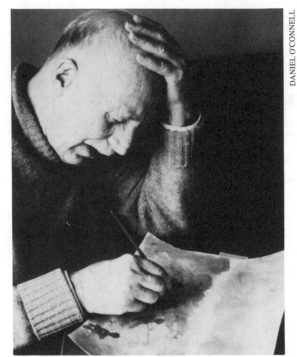

DANIEL O'CONNELL

A 78-year-old resident of a Massachusetts nursing home involved in water colors.

Special Programs for Older People

Others prefer special programs, often held elsewhere on a campus. When working with them we may use similar media, but teaching them is different from our experiences teaching younger students. Most young college students seem to be willing to sit still in class and listen as professors spout this or that, whereas many older people want to take part in discussions rather than be lectured to. And they seek active involvement with art media as well as art history and art appreciation.[4] Other special programs for the elderly are found in the community at "Y's" senior centers, religious centers, museums, and other sites. As always, different people prefer different approaches to arts classes in terms of their comfort and attitudes toward working with their own age cohorts.

Training Leaders

With the growth of special programs for older adults, it is imperative that colleges and universities incorporate material on the arts and the elderly in the methodology courses which future arts teachers take. New courses in the visual arts are needed, geared to those who are teaching or will teach the arts to older adults. In addition, materials and programs need to be made available for gerontologists and recreation directors, since both groups will be called upon to organize programs as well as to hire those who will be the teachers.

There is still another group of practitioners whom we need to reach. They are the people who lack an arts background, but who have been leading the visual arts and/or arts and crafts programs for years in senior centers, hospitals, nursing homes, and other health-related facilities. Now that settings where elderly congregate are gaining attention, these programs are being scrutinized and sometimes found wanting. We must attract these practitioners back to the college setting or some other in-service course work to enhance their experiences and allow them some degree of re-tooling. We have much to learn from these leaders about working with older adults, but they are in need of learning which will permit them to set standards of excellence in their arts program.

Many programs developed in the recent past were often geared toward copy work or kits, or junk-made-into-more-junk because employees had little or no visual arts background. This was due in part to lack of adequate funds; professionals demand higher salaries. But there was also a lack of awareness on the part of administrators, such as activities directors, regarding the proper content of a quality visual arts program.

We also must address our program to college students in gerontology as well as recreation and leisure studies who desire background in the arts. They need courses which will assist them to run arts programs, or at least to learn enough to hire the right persons to do this, i.e. art educators with background in working with the elderly.

Add to the list the art educators with years of background in working with children who are now ready and willing to switch to the older population, and the new art educators who know at the start of their careers that they want to work with older people "teaching" arts and crafts.

You can see the tremendous task ahead of us. Donald Hoffman has pointed out the many different people now involved in developing arts programs who need to increase their art skills.[5] He also notes the problem that has arisen as to just who should teach the arts. Should they be qualified artist/educator or recreation directors or aging practitioners or volunteers (who may or may not have the background in the arts)? I agree with his decision that artist/educators are the best qualified in terms of knowledge and ability in art, but these and others interested in working in the arts with the elderly will benefit from arts training and gerontology courses, all of which will be shared with the elderly in the long run.

Methodology

With the Well Elderly

The well elderly are not passive learners; they need to and want to share in the planning, organizing, and implementing as well as the evaluation of their programs.[6] An art teacher working with them will need to identify the leisure patterns of the given group, their depth of previous arts involvement and preferences, and attitudes toward experimentation and toward the arts in general. Are they willing to take chances in a supportive atmosphere? What are the components of a supportive atmosphere? When is the best time for a program to be offered? How often, and how long should it be?[7]

Participants in an art center need to be assisted in seeing that what they are doing is worth doing. We must avoid trivia! When an artist works in a studio, it is serious business. Naturally, not everyone who comes to such classes will develop this attitude of seriousness, but it should be in the air to avoid making it just another way to pass the time. Different kinds of art programs will appeal to different people. In addition, different requirements must be met, such as adequate light for those who may have eye problems, clarity of presentation for those with hearing impairment, and adaptations of the tools needed to create for those with physical disabilities involving arms and hands.

People are often coaxed into taking part in different recreational activities prior to lunch or after it is served at nutrition centers. Here opportunities to develop new skills, or to pick up on old ones, are made available in settings where everyone feels "at home." And it is here that quality programs will inspire some to find a new approach to life through different creative opportunities.

Although we tend to think of involvement in the arts as a socialization experience, specifically in the visual arts it is likely that some will prefer working individually, away from the crowd. Many will work on a painting within the class or studio setting, but we need to allow for the possibility that once techniques have reached a certain degree of mastery, some will prefer working alone, with the art teacher offering advice as requested.

In crafts, people have tended to work in groups—a quilting bee is one example from the past. While knitting or crocheting, people who know what they are doing seem free to chat. Weavers can work alone or in a bustling studio, as can jewelers. They usually plan their designs in advance and then follow the plan. The manner of working will depend on the medium used and the personality of the people involved.

Working with crafts materials sometimes seems easier to people who are new to the arts. But crafts often come with "crutches" in the form of kits. These are someone's ideas which require that one knows how to follow directions, but which allow little personal creativity or thinking. This is perhaps why such crafts appear as heavily as they do in programs for elders. What we have been calling the fine arts require giving of oneself, and exposing oneself much more than may at first be comfortable. This is true as well of creative work in some of the craft areas, but they do appear to be less threatening to many people.

Therefore I believe that it may be best to start people new to the arts with simple crafts experiences – aim for success, but with integrity. So often recreation programs at senior centers and "Y's" emphasize kits; people get bored and stop attending these classes, but some come because they have little else to do and this occupies them for a time. Bad habits often result. It is difficult to wean people away once they start to copy rather than create.

Practical Considerations

We must develop any number of different art curricula to meet the unique needs of various populations. But there are certain aspects which everyone working with the elderly must keep in mind. Although many in this last phase of life remain as able as ever, some cannot hear, see, or move as well as they used to. We must be certain that the area is well lighted. Write in a large clear hand on the chalkboard, and when you speak, look directly at the students. When on a field trip, allow time to get from here to there, as it will probably take longer than when touring with younger students. Avoid a patronizing manner. Speak a little louder, but do not shout. Find out what the students think about in response to what they see. Offer good criticism but be supportive at the same time. It would seem that these teaching strategies are important no matter what the age of our students, but particularly important for the older student.

Those preparing to teach art to older people must take a number of courses in addition to the art methodology being discussed here. They need background information in sociological, biological, and physiological aspects of aging. To assume that this material can be included in an art course is to give it much less importance than it deserves; to assume there is time in an art methodology course to do this and include adequate art experiences and background as well, would be absurd.

Let us now clarify some of the settings and possible course content as they now exist in locations where elderly can find arts courses available to them.

College Campus

Elderly join the regular students in both studio, lecture, and art history courses. There is no attempt to change these courses in any way. The professors work with the entire class, and also with individuals, in planning the work for the semester; the elderly become regular students and do the course work as required: (available day and night).

Adult Education

These classes might have students ranging from sixteen to ninety-nine. Available only at night, this factor might keep some elderly away as they tend to prefer daytime classes. Once again, the teacher needs to introduce the basic course content, then work with individuals who develop their own style, be it in painting, sculpture, ceramics, jewelry, weaving, or drawing. Night school teachers have been working with this wide range of students for a very long time, as it was the only place people could study at low cost in a school setting close to home. Students who opt for a given studio course tend to know by word-of-mouth what it will offer, such as a good teacher, or an interesting medium, or both. They do not expect a watered-down curriculum.

Local "Y"

These tend to be similar to night school classes, but are available both day and night. There are two possible approaches: segregated classes for the elderly, or mixed-age classes open to everyone. This depends on who is hired to run the arts and crafts as well as studio courses.

Senior Centers

These may be located on a college campus, the local church or synagogue, or some center-city buildings easily accessible via public transportation, if at all possible. The community center is often arranged around a lunch program, and called a nutrition site. Those attending the nutrition centers often come to socialize and to eat. They play cards, crochet, and chat while awaiting lunch. When art is available, such a program faces a lot of competition and requires a very strong and well-qualified teacher to attract and involve people.

Other senior centers, where the lunch is not the prime reason for its existence, such as those on a college campus, can offer high-quality programs with excellent course choices. There is usually a lounging area where people can socialize, and this is one way they find out which courses and teachers are good. There is often an atmosphere conducive to learning and working.

In Nursing Homes, Hospitals, and Health Related Facilities

As people live longer, there is an increasing number of idle disabled for whom programs must be developed. Add to them the isolated who may not be physically disabled, but yet cannot get themselves out and involved with community programs. The psychological mind-set of these people is that they cannot learn.[8] Over half of them are not interested in any kind of education; they do not believe there is anything they can do.

We need to inspire these disabled or isolated people to be involved. We have to help them find out what they can do, so that they can continue to feel capable at least in some small ways at the start.[9]

Many do begin to feel better when they are involved in cultural programs because it takes their minds away from their aches and pains and replaces these with other concerns.

For example, when a group of nursing home residents were given the responsibility for matters such as decorating their rooms, they became more alert, active, and happier.[10] I am convinced that, given the right opportunities, these and many other disabled elderly can do quality art work as well. Those who have worked with them know this is possible. If you expect more of people, if you give them selected challenges and support, they will become happier participants!

Those in health related facilities are mobile and can get around both inside and out of the facility. Some may be very interested in some phase of art, attend museums and galleries, and generally live as though they were still at home, with only some limitations due to physical problems.

Those in the nursing homes and hospitals are usually in wheelchairs, or need walkers. This sets limits on how freely they can move around the facility to take part in different activities. They are often tranquilized and unable to become truly involved. However, given a quality program, rewarding things can happen: people snap out of their lethargy and function on a surprisingly competent level. They can then use a number of different art media and create quality works. This caliber of program is rarely available since the tendency is to assume they cannot do anything and expectations are low. Once one has seen what is really possible, it is shocking to realize how few people in these facilities have the chance to be creative. Yet we know many could be, if given the opportunity. One imperative is that qualified art educators must be hired as the teachers; they have the know-how to inspire people to function adequately and to try to create quality works.

I have visited all of the types of sites noted here, and there is one thing that was easily observable: wherever there was a qualified person in charge of the program, quality work was going on. This is true even for the frail, ill elderly with limited mobility. A good art teacher knows how to work with each person to bring out his or her best. An activities director who has an art background can offer in-service experiences to the staff and this makes for better quality programming as well.

Approaches to Programming

Many settings could offer in-depth exposure in one or another specific art media. A beginner's ceramics class introduces students to working with clay, and an advanced class allows them to work at their own pace, once they have learned the techniques. But in some settings, both advanced and beginning students work together, learning from each other. This depends on the number of interested students, space availability, and adequate funding to pay a ceramics teacher for more than the one class.

Some organizations like to start people off with a general arts and crafts course in which they get to try a number of different media. From this experience, they can decide which area they want to work with in-depth. The next group of courses should offer those media the students found to be of greatest interest, so that they can continue to work in their chosen medium. Once they gain the necessary skills and know-how, these students should be given the opportunity to work individually. Thus a workshop atmosphere exists in the art studio, allowing for individual advancement and a wide range of possible choices. This attracts people who do not like to be kept waiting in a step-by-step approach. This makes it possible for those with different levels of functioning to be in the same course.

Those of us who have been involved with the arts have seen the positive responses of our students when given opportunities to function creatively. We know it is not always easy, but if we keep trying, we can have some degree of success. It would be useful to clarify that while elderly students may be thinking of the best ways to use their leisure hours, they may find themselves involved in an art medium to the extent that they become true practitioners—it *can* happen and does, for some people.

At first, you may want to show slides with a range of styles in drawing, painting, construction (clay, wood), and crafts (jewelry, fibers, ceramics). Choose work that ranges from quite Realistic to Primitive to Nonobjective, showing successful works in all styles. This will help people feel more comfortable regarding what they believe they can or cannot accomplish with art materials. Showing only very Realistic works will cause some to feel inadequate. They cannot possibly do that kind of work, or so they believe; therefore it is not for them. Showing only Primitive works will lead others to assume you think little of their abilities. Try to include some slides of elderly professional artists, as well as those who have recently become involved with art. We know that artists need never retire—they just keep on creating as long as they live! Use this as a way to inspire potential art students.

Present more than one way of working and more than one medium, if possible. For example, crafts, as noted earlier, seem less threatening as a starting point for some. If you choose fibers as one of your media, include ways of working that will attract men as well as women. Avoid sex-segregated classes, as the areas that attract women begin to be less valued by the women than those that attract both men and women.

People are sometimes motivated to create works which can become gifts. While this should not be the only reason for holding such classes, it may be one way of getting started. Both men and women could weave belts or guitar straps. Place mats are not only the province of women, nor are wall hangings or bookmarks. Such practical weaving basics get people involved. They can work at home as well as in the art studio. They can make color and design decisions once they learn the simple weaving skills. After these introductory sessions, students with an interest in weaving can begin to think creatively about this medium and develop their own unique forms.

A class in which a variety of media have been introduced allows students to choose the area of greatest interest. Some may opt for involvement in drawing, painting, claywork, woodwork. A qualified art teacher can shift from area to area, medium to medium, with ease. The only limitation is space, class time, availability of supplies, and interested students. Some elderly students say "What am I going to do with it? What do I need it for?" They need to learn that it is the process of creating that is important, not always the final product. When the product happens to be a satisfactory piece of work, that is an added bonus. In many programs, emphasis is only on the product. After a few weeks of working, it is important to look over what has been produced and discuss with each student some new directions.

Exhibitions of works completed—displayed with taste—will attract new students and enhance the reputations of those already involved. For students to begin to function as artists, they must realize that not everything they make

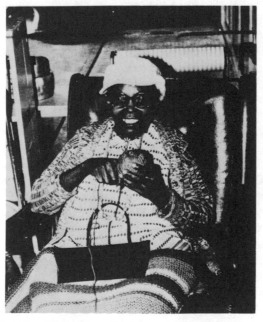

MURRAY GREENBERG

East Orange Nursing Home, New Jersey.

will be worth exhibiting, nor possibly even worth keeping. A portfolio for each student is the best way to save works, with dates on each piece. This allows both the teacher and the student to begin to see growth and development. Emphasis should not be toward exhibiting, but toward artistic involvement. Art entails introspection and students, once they realize this for themselves, will begin to work at their own pace, no longer in need of constant teacher attention at each step. This attracts people who do not like to be kept waiting for the slower students to catch up. Once we discover their interests, overcome fears, inspire confidence in taking risks, we can develop programs to meet those interests.

We are working with a diverse population which cannot be served by one simple curriculum. Rather, we have to study people's needs and build a curriculum based upon them. It must constantly change and grow to suit our elder students wherever we meet them.

NOTES

[1]Atchley, R.C. *The social forces in later life,* Wadsworth, California.

[2]Kaplan, M. The arts in an aging population from the conference *The Aging of America,* University of Delaware, November 1977.

[3]Covington, J.P. Toward a philosophical base for community arts—The museum role in *Lifelong learning and the arts* Hoffman, Greenberg, & Fitzner, Reston, Virginia: National Art Education Association, 1980.

[4]Kaplan, M. The arts in an aging population from the conference *The Aging of America,* University of Delaware, November 1977.

[5]Hoffman, D. Training personnel for work with the elderly in: *Lifelong Learning and the Visual Arts,* Hoffman, et al. editors National Art Education Association.

[6]Barnes, C. Geragogy: The education of older adults San Francisco, California: National Art Education Association Convention, April 1979.

[7]Hoffman, D. *The elderly and the arts,* unpublished manuscript, 1977.

[8]Barnes, C. Geragogy: The education of older adults San Francisco, California: National Art Education Association, April 1979.

[9]Berghorn, F.J., Shafer, D.E., Steere, G.H., & Wiseman, R.F.,*The urban elderly—A study of life satisfaction!* New York: Landmark Studies, Allanheld Osmun/Universe Books, 1978.

[10]Wack J., & Rodin, J. The nursing home gulag *Psychology Today,* July 1979, Vol. 13 #2.

SUGGESTED READINGS

Comfort, A. *A good age.* New York: Simon & Schuster, 1976.

Jones, J.E. *On teaching art to the elderly: Research & practice,* NAES Convention papers, San Francisco, April 1979.

Newman, T.R. *Contemporary African arts & crafts.* New York: Crown Publishers, 1974.

Sunderland, J.T. *Older Americans and the arts: A human equation.* Washington D.C.: National Council on Aging, 1976.

Fruit Hill Day Care Center, Rhode Island.

I was delighted by his imagination, his sense of humor, and his own unrestrained expression of excitement at his accomplishment.

Gail Porter, B.A. Photography; is a graduate of the Rhode Island School of Design. She was Photographer-in-Residence for the Rhode Island State Council on the Arts, 1980-82. Ms. Porter conducts workshops for a variety of populations, including senior adults, troubled adolescents and young children. Former teaching appointments were at the Archeological Society in Jerusalem, Israel, and Phillips Exeter Academy.

FOCUSING
PHOTOGRAPHY WITH SENIORS

Gail Porter

The photography workshop took place in a day-care center for the elderly. We had about eight to twelve regular participants working with my assistant and me 2 hours weekly. A crafts room with an equipped darkroom adjoining it provided our main work evironment.

Introducing a New Skill

I planned it as a hands-on experience which would introduce the participants to the basics of photography: basic design concepts; how photosensitive materials work; how a camera works; and how negatives and prints are made. These goals are common for most beginning photography courses. More important, for our programs, was the underlying purpose of helping the participants believe that they are vital individuals capable of experiencing and learning new ideas and processes. There was an undertone of fear at trying something new. To help them overcome it required consistent attention. *Revitalizing confidence* was my first and main work each week.

Fear was expressed in many ways:

"I don't feel well."
"The smell of chemicals gives me a headache."
"I get dizzy in the darkroom."

"You poor dear, trying to teach us old people."
"I'm not an artist; I can't do this."
"We're too old to learn."

But as the workshops progressed, I found the group showed increased willingness to try new techniques.

A Way to Begin

I began most sessions with a few minutes of simple stretching and movement exercises which can be done sitting or standing. Movements were often suggested by the participants. We also did some eye exercises such as "Close your eyes, look to the left; open your eyes. What is the first thing you see?" This helps to stimulate visual awareness as well as an awareness of oneself and others within an environment.

A weekly assignment was to come to class prepared to tell about something which one had not noticed before. I found that this sharing at the beginning of a class enabled all to participate fully. It opened communication channels between the members of the group and me.

What are Photograms?*

During the first few classes I showed slides and photographs in books to illustrate design concepts. Then each participant made a photogram which emphasized shape, pattern, and texture. This was a first introduction to a light-sensitive material. Later we used Polaroid and Diana cameras for instant feedback to check what we were seeing. Group members helped each other develop film from the Diana cameras and print it in the Center's darkroom. We expanded the possibilities. Photograms became postcards. Portraits without faces were tried. We made a large collage with photograms, photographs, and prose/poetry.

The postcard class was one of the highlights of the project. Everyone had made a photogram the week before. I brought in many postcards, some of them handmade, and a rubber stamp which printed "postcard." I drew an enlarged mock-up of the back of a postcard and asked the group to make their photograms into cards by drawing the elements on the back of the paper and including a place for the postage stamps. The name of the artist was to be included as well.

One man, who is losing his vision, traced a circle with a nickel for the

---

*A photogram is a shadowy image produced without a camera by placing an object directly on photopaper, exposing all of it to light and developing the paper. The shapes of the objects will be emphasized. The degree of translucency and texture of the objects and the strength and direction of the light source will determine the gradation of printed tones from black through gray to white. (*See* Notes) postmark. He did this largely from touch. Almost within the circle he printed the letters "Prov. R. I." and drew wavy lines across it as a postal mark. He was extremely excited by the fact that he had this wonderful idea and that he carried it through even though he could barely see.

"I'm Thinking of You"

Everyone wrote a message to a spouse, a child, or friend on their postcards and addressed them. The man who drew the previously mentioned postmark used the image of a key on his photogram. On the back, a note to his son read, "Did you say you lost your keys?"

I was delighted by his imagination, his sense of humor, and his own unrestrained expression of excitement at his accomplishment. I also sensed that most people in the class did not usually communicate through the mails. The idea of making a card to send to a loved one for no other purpose than to say "I'm thinking of you," was novel to them. At the end of this workshop the entire group walked to the nearest mailbox.

A Different Pace

I learned that activities take longer with older people. There was a different pace at the center than in my own life. Flexibility in planning, extra patience, love, and much individual attention were constantly needed.

For example, one man complained bitterly about working in the darkroom. I offered him the choice of developing film during that workshop or printing it the next week. He chose to develop the film that day so he would be in the dark only long enough to load the film into the tank. The rest of the process could be done in full light. The following week I showed him the negatives he had made and invited him into the darkroom to watch someone else make a print from them. He ended up staying in the darkroom until he had the opportunity to make a print himself.

The photography workshops offered to all participants an opportunity for personal growth. I too changed. I began to understand better the people with whom I worked.

The Rewards

At the end of the project I received many responses. Many said "Thank you for a very interesting class." Others exclaimed over what they had done, "I've never taken a photograph before and here it is! It's pretty good!" One woman said, "This is the first time I've ever seen pictures made. I didn't think I could do it!" And the man referred to earlier said "I can't see very well, but look at this picture I just printed!"

NOTES

*Photograms

Materials Required:

1 Box Studio Proof paper, 8 x 10"
1 Piece of cardboard for each student
1 Piece of glass for each student
Kodak Fixer to make 1 quart
2 buckets or wash tubs
Line and clothespins
"Found objects," including things transparent, opaque, translucent

Mix Fixer according to direction. Then dilute it with 1 quart additional water. Put in one bucket. Fill second bucket with water.

Cut paper to appropriate size. Put paper on cardboard, object on paper; cover with glass. Go into the sun for about 1 minute until paper turns dark purple, almost brown. If light is bright overcast, stay outside until paper gets dark. If weather is not sunny, use photo flood light #1.

Finally, return objects to where they go. Put photo paper into Fixer until it turns brown; then into water. When finished, carefully rinse prints in 5 changes of water. Hang to dry.

Save fixer in one-half gallon bottle for up to 3 months.

SUGGESTED READINGS

The camera cookbook. Workshop for Learning Things. 5 Bridge Street, Watertown, Massachusetts 02172.

Dufault, J. Vintage: The bold survivors. New York: Pilgrim Press, 1978 (42 photos).

Harelson, R. SWAK: The complete book of mail fun for kids. New York: Workman Publishing, 1981.

Kohn, E. Photography: A manual for shutterbugs. Englewood Cliffs: Prentice Hall, 1965.

Steichen, E. The family of man. New York: The Museum of Modern Art, 1955.

PART VII

ADMINISTRATORS AND EDUCATORS SPEAK

The future impact of creative arts leaders now pioneering in work with the elderly will be largely determined by the significance given their programs by geriatric administrators, educators, governmental lawmakers—county, state and national—and the general citizenry.

Toward this end, we invited a cross section of administrators and educators to respond to a number of questions. We asked them to assess the values they place on the role of the arts in light of their institutional priorities. The unanimous response favored expressive and therapeutic arts opportunitites for the well and ill. They endorsed proliferation of creative arts leadership and training to enhance the quality of long lives. In addition, some of the respondents described innovative arts programs they offer older adults in their facilities.

In the section that follows, we offer you a selection of the responses from:

1) A college gerontology center for students and working professionals;
2) A training program in a home for the aged which offers continuing education credits for geriatric workers from nursing homes and community;
3) A community-based arts center with outreach programs in nursing homes;
4) Three nursing homes.

1)From: Robert A. Famighetti, Director, Gerontology Center, Kean College of New Jersey, Union, N.J.

Question: What values do you see in creative arts programming for older adults?
Response: Although the therapeutic value of creative arts programming must be underscored, we, as professionals in the field of gerontology, often neglect to realize the other perhaps more important values of the arts with older adults. For example, the arts can become the language of the aged, a language created over the course of a person's life. The arts can speak for all an older person has been, is, can be, and can continue to become.

The human values, furthermore, of self-expression, creativity, and compassion are often lost in our arts programming because of immediate work goals and somewhat limited professional knowledge of the arts and of aging.

The creative arts as an expression of humanity is an inseparable tenet in the lives of older persons. Unfortunately, this has been a relatively unknown and neglected quality in the human services system which primarily focuses on the material needs of the aging.

The arts embody the expression of human freedom; timeless, spaceless, and limitless, the creative arts can provide meaning as the link between the aging human and a world seemingly uninterested in listening and understanding.

Question: Among the many urgently needed physical and psychological areas to be addressed by your training workshops, why do you offer training in the arts and arts therapies for geriatric workers on all levels? How do you hope this training will affect workers?
Response: Most personnel until recently possessed little or no formal training in gerontology and performed their work with fairly stereotypic values about the aged. The same is often true of arts personnel.

Historically, training for personnel in the field of gerontology has been a focus of the federal, state, and local governments since the 1961 White House Conference on Aging. Each succeeding WHCOA, most recently the 1981 Conference in Washington, has emphasized the importance of education and training directives. The reports of these conferences have called for education about aging at all levels of society, education for older adults, and education for personnel who work with the aging. Since 1961 much has been accomplished; much more needs to be done.

The Older Americans Act, a landmark piece of legislation enacted in 1965, provided for personnel training in aging through Title IV-A funds. During the 1970s these monies were plentiful, with millions of dollars available each year to train gerontology personnel. The 1980s has seen and will continue to experience massive cuts in these funds.

As a director of a college gerontology center, I have been fortunate to have such Title IV-A funding to provide training since 1978. Considering the limited funding now available, diverse training needs and equally diverse levels of personnel, how does one determine the priorities?

If creative arts programming is seen as a therapeutic intervention, then available training monies can be utilized to train arts personnel. If such programming is not viewed as therapeutic modality, (and this does not negate my answer to the earlier question; it only underscores the realities of our world), the current priority of the creative arts for training would be greatly diminished.

Individuals who are preparing to work with older persons must be provided with accurate information about the aging process and issues affecting the aged as well as the nature of creative programming and other aspects of arts programming.

The need for training by arts personnel addresses all of the above. Arts specialists who also are insightful about the aging adult can help us break with the invalid assumptions and generalities normally associated with age; develop an appreciation of older persons as a resource and as creative participants in society. Arts personnel can lead us to appreciate and address individuality and wide-ranging abilities, attitudes and interests.

2) From: Mrs. Lilly Miller, Director of Continuing Education, Goldfarb Institute; Educational Coordinator, Central New Jersey Jewish Home for the Aged.

Question: What is your major role?
Response: I organize and supervise training programs for our staff and for activity directors, social workers, nurses, supervisors, administrators, therapists and other geriatric workers of the state. Courses are usually scheduled in our facilities, and occasionally at a nearby college, or at other long-term-care facilities. CEU's are issued for all our courses. (A CEU is a nationally recognized unit of credit for Continuing Education courses. Ten instructional hours equal one CEU.)

Each year, in addition to courses addressing physical and psychological needs for the elderly, I include 1-day programs of dance, drama, music, visual arts, and arts and crafts. The specialists who lead these courses are recognized in their fields as artist/teachers or therapists, and as professionals who know how to adapt their philosophies and techniques to the needs of older adults in nursing homes and community sites.

Question: How do you identify a creative arts activity? And what values does it serve?
Response: Have you ever visited an activity program in a nursing home and

seen a group of residents making pretty yarn balls, tile trivets, and stuffed animals, or coloring pictures by numbers?

These may be valid programs to improve gross and fine motor control. But let us all beware of professionals—teachers, leaders or therapists—who equate busy skills and physical therapy with creative activities.

What do I consider creative activity? To me, these can include involvement with language (prose, poetry, life journals); music (vocal, choral, instrumental, appreciation); media (photography, video, television, radio—instruments of potential self-expression rather than passive experience); drama (creative drama, theatre games, drama as therapy, plays, performance, and reader's theatre); art (drawing, painting, sculpture, ceramics, and other crafts).

Creative activities are rejuvenating to the mind and spirit as well as the body. They provide opportunities for new experiences, personal expression, personal exploration, and lots of room for imagination and original ideas. They offer open-ended arts problems that challenge new solutions. There is always a basic structure within which to work. But the end result is not prescribed by someone else in a pre-set "recipe."

Creativity is synonymous with playfulness. And this often is a quality that lies dormant in older individuals. Yet from childhood on, "play" is a vital way to explore the world. It implies taking risks, chancing failure; deep involvement in examining ideas and materials; the ability to project into new possibilities. In the creative arts we can walk old or new routes in new ways. They offer opportunities for great delight as any peak experiences can do.

Question: Where do you begin in orienting activity or program directors to these values if they have not known them before?
Response: We start by asking a number of questions: What would you like to do with your leisure time in your own "golden years"? How do you plan an overall program for the older persons with whom you work? How do you decide what to offer them? Do you consider their interests and needs, or does your hidden agenda influence your plans for them? Do you attempt to transplant program ideas and activities that have been successful in other facilities or do you adapt and plan for individual participation? How do you reinforce success for each participant in your programs? And finally, we ask what these professionals understand as the "creative process."

For creativity to occur in a program, leaders must understand it through their own subjective experiences. But first we address their individual attitudes, and early in-service workshops center on:

value clarification—self-assessment of attitudes toward aging, illness, and death;

discussion of the myths of aging and ageism in our society;
sensitivity training – experiential exercises to simulate sensory, personal, and role losses.

For those involved with institutionalized elderly, in-service programs should also include content on family systems and relationships, decision-making processes by a resident and his or her family in regard to entering an institution; the impact of moving into and coping with an institutional setting.

In institutional or community settings, it is essential to develop an understanding, in all staff members, of the importance and meanings of ethnic and cultural customs and religious backgrounds.

Question: With this rich background achieved, what is your next step?
Response: Then, I believe, the staff professional is ready to consider arts approaches, philosophies, materials, and resources. I ask our arts specialists to present a blend of theory and specific activities. By active participation in these exercises or activities I find that our course participants can *experience* the meanings. Our arts specialists also demonstrate how a creative environment is built which encourages creative expression. In many of our courses, we try to stress the need for a sense of humor; the willingness of geriatric leaders to practice self-criticism; also the importance of listening, and observing the responses of each unique older person in workshops in order to determine what activities to introduce and what encouragement, support and approval each person needs to "open up" to his or her expressive potential.

3) From: Mr. Daniel M. O'Connell, Artistic Director and Fund-Raiser, Berkshire Artisans Gallery and Workshop, Pittsfield, Massachusetts.

Question: What is the Berkshire Artisans Gallery?
Response: We are a community arts center, located in a large, center-city store with easy access for handicapped elderly. We offer workshops in painting, drawing, sculpture, photo-silkscreen, photography, pottery, weaving, batik and tie-dyeing, dance, mime, and music history to local residents of all ages. We serve approximately 350 older adults from the Neighborhood Strategy Area – an area designated by the Housing and Urban Development Agency (HUD) for low-income housing to serve the handicapped and elderly of Pittsfield. We are part of the City of Pittsfield and are supervised by the Pittsfield Council on Aging. All our programs are free for persons over fifty-five. We start at that age to prepare more people for their retirement, at the same time that we are serving those already retired.

The Artisans, which incidentally means "skilled older craftsmen," serves, as well, as the base from which outreach workers bring the arts to people confined in nursing homes. We also exhibit art work by the older artists—in our gallery, in nursing homes, nutrition sites, banks, department stores, and restaurants.

Our funding comes from the National Endowment on the Arts, the Massachusetts Council on the Arts and Humanities, The Campaign for Human Development of the Catholic Conference of Bishops, Title V—Senior Aid Program, Berkshire Home Care Corporation, major corporations, and private donors.

Question: Who are your teachers?
Response: We have 15 artist-teachers—all professionals in their disciplines. In preparing them to work with elderly in our center and in nursing homes, they study a manual we have developed. There is *no age* in our classes; all are the same age. A basic tenet which makes it possible for anyone to work here is: *we don't do art; we do the best we can.*

The teachers say that they learn about themselves by working with older people. And they set a tone for the class that lets things happen. They strive to lead individuals to develop their own unique approaches for a truly creative effort.

Question: What human needs do you feel the arts can fill? In other words, what are the benefits of your program for the elderly?
Response: Ours is the only program of its kind in New England. Other programs, as at senior centers, are nice, but the focus is on doing things *for* the elderly, and *to* them. Egg-carton art, popsicle art, all predesigned for a specific result.

We say that art is work. People come to be involved. This changes peoples' self-concept. There are many people who want to learn and to do, not to sit around being entertained. We offer the older adult choices.

We see exuberance; personal dignity returns. Too often programs in institutions strip people of their dignity; then their attention span becomes limited. Here they work as members of a group. We have brought our older artists off the back-burner into the mainstream of the community.

Additionally, we are concerned with how the community views the elderly. Older people have been respected, but not considered to have any value or worth. One way we do this is by exhibiting their art work to show the community what they can do. Right now, at Howard Johnson's Restaurant is an exhibit by a man of eighty-seven. He came into the nursing home paralyzed and depressed. He used to paint. He is unable to handle oils in the Home so we introduced him to water colors. His depression lifted; he is productive again.

What we are offering is serious art. Our exhibitions are judged. Our touring art shows go into nursing homes to change their community rooms into galleries. We also bring in professional artists to give lectures on these exhibits.

From our early dance-mime workshops in nursing homes, we moved handicapped dancers in wheelchairs out to do a combined program with the Berkshire Ballet Company—again, to show the community that older adults in wheelchairs in their own way can dance too.

Question: Is there a special project in-work you would like to speak about?
Response: Yes, we are working in nursing homes on a film for Polaroid. The film will be a history lesson told by older people, to be shared with school children. We give the residents cameras and film. They record their life histories. Right now we are concentrating on two subjects: neighborhoods and entertainment, yesterday and today. They start by photographing each other, nurses, life in the Home. Then I take them back to the neighborhoods they came from and we photograph the changes in the area, and talk about them.

Question: What new programs do you plan for the future?
Response: We want to build our music program. We have a composer who has joined us to lead two courses: Gateway to Music and Baroque Music History. That's a start. We hope to add more.

4)From: Audrey DuPont, Activities Director, Briarcliffe Health Care Facility, Johnston, Rhode Island.

Question: What arts activities do you schedule?
Response: We regularly schedule arts and crafts, ceramics, chorus, drama, and painting. Some of our residents perform in a chorus that tours to other homes and public places. I would like to add creative writing, storytelling, poetry, and drama with more groups. Most of our people are from the blue-collar work force with very strong work ethics, little idea of hobbies or other forms of leisure activities.

Question: Do your leaders receive arts/art therapy training?
Response: All of our leaders have had some training in the arts. The arts and crafts person is a pharmacist, perhaps less trained than some, but he does have a therapeutic personality. One leader has a degree in music and has

almost completed her Gerontology degree. The ceramics teacher is a graduate of the Rhode Island School of Design and we have a part-time drama leader.

Question: What values do you see in creative arts programming for older adults? What do you believe it can contribute to behavioral change?
Response: The creative arts contribute to the quality of life. They help a person regain some sense of self-worth. I wish we had the staff to reach all of our 120 residents. Interaction in social groups is improved by the arts process. The staff attitude changes then, as well, providing a happier environment for everybody.

Question: What are some of the needs of the elderly that are served by arts programs?
Response: They get a chance to express themselves in ways they cannot do otherwise in a normal day at the Home. The arts also allow many who have difficulty verbalizing the opportunity to show inner feelings. Many who are unable to speak (aphasic) can sing; even an Alzheimer's patient can sing.

5) From: Jeanette DelPadre, Program Coordinator, Scalabrini Nursing Home, North Kingston, Rhode Island.

Question: What arts activities do you schedule?
Response: Two thirds of our population come from ethnic backgrounds and they say they have worked hard in the past and only want to rest and practice their religion. They are afraid that any form of *play* is foolishness. I think that drama and fantasy and music offer them safe ways to vent their feelings, but we have to find the right buttons to push that make them comfortable about laughing and enjoying life more. We have to let them know it's okay to have fun. They can allow themselves to have a good time—they have the right! Music generally appeals to all of them. I bring in artists from the State Council on the Arts to lead workshops. I hire professional performers to entertain, when possible.

Question: Do your leaders receive arts/art therapy training?
Response: Not frequently. The problem I have, as program coordinator for 70 people, is dependence on students and volunteers to carry out the activities I plan. While this is good for program expansion, I cannot expect volunteers to work as staff, assuming staff members' responsibilities. Without enough staff, I cannot train people or have them trained for the tasks I would like to implement. I find my own time and energy must meet the residents' basic needs: shopping, learning to cope with their new life-styles, etcetera. If I could get beyond that, I would be able to build more creative programming.

Question: What values do you see in creative arts programming for older adults? What do you believe it can contribute to behavioral change?

Response: Residents need to express their feelings of loneliness, disappointments, and unfulfilled accomplishments as well as their happinesses. As I mentioned before, I have seen that drama and fantasy and music offer safe ways to vent these feelings.

Arts programs should be ongoing, consistent, and dependably led. Residents need to know programs will continue. Once both program and consistency is intact, then a plan or approach that addresses behavioral change can be implemented for each resident. This will happen best when people are given the opportunity to carry on their lives much as they did before entering the home.

Question: What are some of the needs of the elderly that are served by arts programs?

Response: The creative arts and art therapies benefit both the resident and staff members. They reach inside to the little girl or boy that is inside all of us, allowing some relief from the stresses of life. They are tools that depend on the skill of the individual; training enhances those skills.

Nursing homes are fashioned after the medical model. This model is not conducive to long-term living. Today many people live a long time in a nursing home and need "living" situations. Nursing addresses the treatment and sick side of the patient; the creative arts address the well side, helping to move the person away from his or her sickness. This is a much healthier way to address long-term living in nursing homes.

6) From: Judes Ziemba, Activity Coordinator and Volunteer Coordinator, Heritage Hall Nursing Home (South Building), Agawam, Massachusetts.

Question: What arts activities do you schedule?

Response: At our facility we offer a variety of arts programs but our most prominent is the Drama Club. It started over three years ago, and we are now preparing for our seventh production.

Last year we started a dollhouse workshop that involved our entire facility. We did it in conjunction with our Occupational Therapy Department. The constructing was done by our woodworking class and the decorating by residents, staff, and volunteers. Color schemes were entirely up to the residents, many of whom also knit the rugs for the house. Our volunteers made curtains and minature paintings for the walls; our staff encouraged the residents and provided a few suggestions. When the project was completed, we put our "prize" on display in the local library and it was so well received that we are now working on our second house!

Another program which has been very successful is our ceramics class. Deep concentration and thought is given to each piece—and the work is displayed in our show-case if it has not already been sold!

I would like to hear more music in the Home; lessons and a choir group or band.

Question: Do your leaders receive arts/art therapy training?
Response: I majored in Theatre Arts and I had my own improvisational theatre group for 6 years. I have attended several theatre workshops to improve my techniques and to keep informed about different methods of acting. I have given drama workshops to activity coordinators in my area.

Question: What values do you see in creative arts programming for older adults? What do you believe it can contribute to behavioral change?
Response: There is so much value in a creative arts program. First of all, it is very therapeutic. Some words that come to mind are: self-esteem, achievement, social interaction, cooperation, teamwork, pride, and dignity. I have seen residents who had lost interest in everything come alive in creative arts programs. I have also seen residents who do not actively participate in our productions but they do attend them and encourage the performers to continue.

Question: What are some of the needs of the elderly that are served by arts programs?
Response: The need to belong and to be loved, to feel an increased sense of well-being, to be a participant and receive acknowledgement for whatever contribution is made, to share knowledge with others, and to be oneself—these are *human* needs, profound, universal—so well served by creative arts programs.

PROFESSIONAL ORGANIZATIONS

American Art Therapy Association, 5999 Stevenson Avenue, Alexandria, Virginia 22304.

American Association of Music Therapy, 66 Morris Avenue, Springfield, N.J. 07081

American Dance Guild, Inc., 1619 Broadway, Suite 603, New York, New York 10019.

American Dance Therapy Association, Inc., 2000 Century Plaza, Suite 230, Columbia, Maryland 21044.

American Psychological Association, Division of Adult Development and Aging, 1200 17th Street, N.W., Washington, D.C. 20036.

American Theatre Association, Senior Adult Theatre Program, 1000 Vermont Avenue, Washington, D.C. 20005.

Association for Poetry Therapy, 799 Broadway Suite 629, New York, New York 10003.

Children's Theatre Association of America (Division of ATA), CTAA Committee for Senior Adult Theatre, 1000 Vermont Avenue, Washington, D.C. 20005.

Encomium Arts Consultants Inc., Rosilyn Wilder, 10 Clairidge Court, Montclair, New Jersey 07042.

Improvise Inc., Creative Drama and Drama Therapy with all ages. Naida Weisberg, P.O. Box 2335, Providence, Rhode Island 02906

National Association of Activity Professionals, P.O. Box 274, Park Ridge, Illinois 60068.

National Association for Drama Therapy, 19 Edward St., New Haven, Conn. 06511

National Association for Music Therapy, 1133 15th St. N.W., Suite 1000, Washington, D.C. 20005

National Center on the Arts and Aging, National Council on Aging, Inc. 600 Maryland Avenue S.W., West Wing 100, Washington, D.C. 20024.

National Committee on Art Education for the Elderly, Albert Beck, Executive Director, 520-5 Culver-Stockton College, Canton, Missouri 63435.

National Council on the Aging, 1828 L Street, N.W., Washington, D.C. 20036.

National Educational Council of Creative Therapies, 20 Rip Road, Hanover, New Hampshire 03755.

National Therapeutic Recreation Society, 1601 North Kent Street, Arlington, Virginia 22209.

INDEX